Olympic Images
1976 Olympic Track and Field
by the Editors of Track and Field News

tafnews
Book Division of Track & Field News

CREDITS

Rick Bayko—57 (lower).

Don Chadez—5, 6, 7, 9, 10, 11, 15, 17 (upper), 18 (right), 19, 20, 21, 22, 23, 26, 27, 28, 29, 30, 31, 32, 33 (lower), 35, 37, 38, 39, 40, 44 (right), 46, 47, 48, 50, 51, 53, 54, 55, 56, 57 (upper), 58, 59, 61 (lower), 62, 63, 65, 68, 71 (lower), 72, 73, 78, 79, 80, 81, 82, 83, 84, 88, 89, 90 (left), 92, 94, 95, 96, 97, 98, 100, 101, 102, 103, 104 (right), 105, 106, 107.

Fred Chez—12.

Rich Clarkson—Cover, Title, 8, 14, 16, 17 (lower), 24, 34, 36, 41, 42, 43, 44 (left), 45, 52, 60, 64, 66, 67, 69, 70, 71 (upper), 74, 76, 87, 90 (right), 91, 93, 99, 109.

Knut Edvard Holm—61 (upper), 77, 85, 104 (left), 108 (lower).

Diane Johnson—25, 33 (upper), 86, 108 (upper).

Bev Junginger—13.

Pat Palazzolo—18 (left).

COVER: Decathlon gold medal winner Bruce Jenner (US).

Published 1977 by Tafnews Press
Book Division of Track & Field News
P.O. Box 296, Los Altos, California 94022 U.S.A.

Standard Book Number 0-911520-75-9

This book was produced by Jon Hendershott and
Ed Fox and the editorial staff of Track & Field News

TO THE
OLYMPIANS
OF MONTREAL

THEY MADE THIS BOOK

The World Arrives

by Garry Hill

Olympic track and field is no longer the exclusive property of the United States. That was the message delivered at Munich. An exclamation point was added at Montreal.

To be sure, the US men still gobbled up the lion's share of top honors, winning three times as many golds as any other country and doubling the score on the USSR on a 10-8-6 . . . basis. And the US women haven't been the dominant force since a strong showing in 1932.

But the gold-medal take has fallen to about half of "normal" in the last two Games and Uncle Sam's men can no longer assume that medals will be "automatic" in most events.

An ardent jingoist will decry this trend and beat his chest in anguish. No need. To repeat an old saw, the US is NOT slipping; it's just that the rest of the world is catching up.

Although the roots of the Games themselves are ancient, track and field as we know it is young, younger even than baseball. The British can claim most of the origins of the sport, which found great popularity in the United States in the late 1800s and early 1900s.

And it stood to reason that a country the size of the US (by far the largest practicing the sport), with its high standard of living and well-developed sporting urges would dominate the Games. Track, in essence, became an *American* sport.

And now, just as the Canadians are discovering what happened when the rest of the world discovered hockey, the US finds itself toppled from the pre-eminent position. And all the Yankee ingenuity in the world isn't going to restore the good old days. Time marches on, although the men aren't marching to the same drummer as the women.

If you are a real track fan, you shouldn't mind the changes. Look at the bright side. Although your favorite American might not win, you are going to see better and better competition, as great talents from all over the world are developed. With the great sprinting traditions of Caribbean nations such as Jamaica and Trinidad, wonder what potential supermen may have preceded Alberto Juantorena in Cuba.

Leave petty ideology aside and revel in the glory of what the highly-trained athletes of the world can do.

The stirrings of the brave new world of track were much in evidence in the men's events at Montreal, as a tasty bouilabaisse of cosmopolitan delight was prepared. (Indeed, one could be snide and comment that the Games were almost as international as an NCAA meet—maybe less, since there were no Kenyans.)

Let's look at the men's winners chronologically: first there was Mexican Daniel Bautista in the walk, the first track and field gold ever won by that country.

Then East Germany's Udo Beyer took the shot.

Then Trinidad's Hasely Crawford took the 100—that country's first-ever gold.

Then the US's Mac Wilkins took the discus.

Then Cuba's Juantorena took the 800—that country's first-ever gold.

Not until the sixth event did we get a repeater, as American Edwin Moses took the 400 hurdles.

Then it was back to the atlas, with Pole Tadeusz Slusarski taking the vault

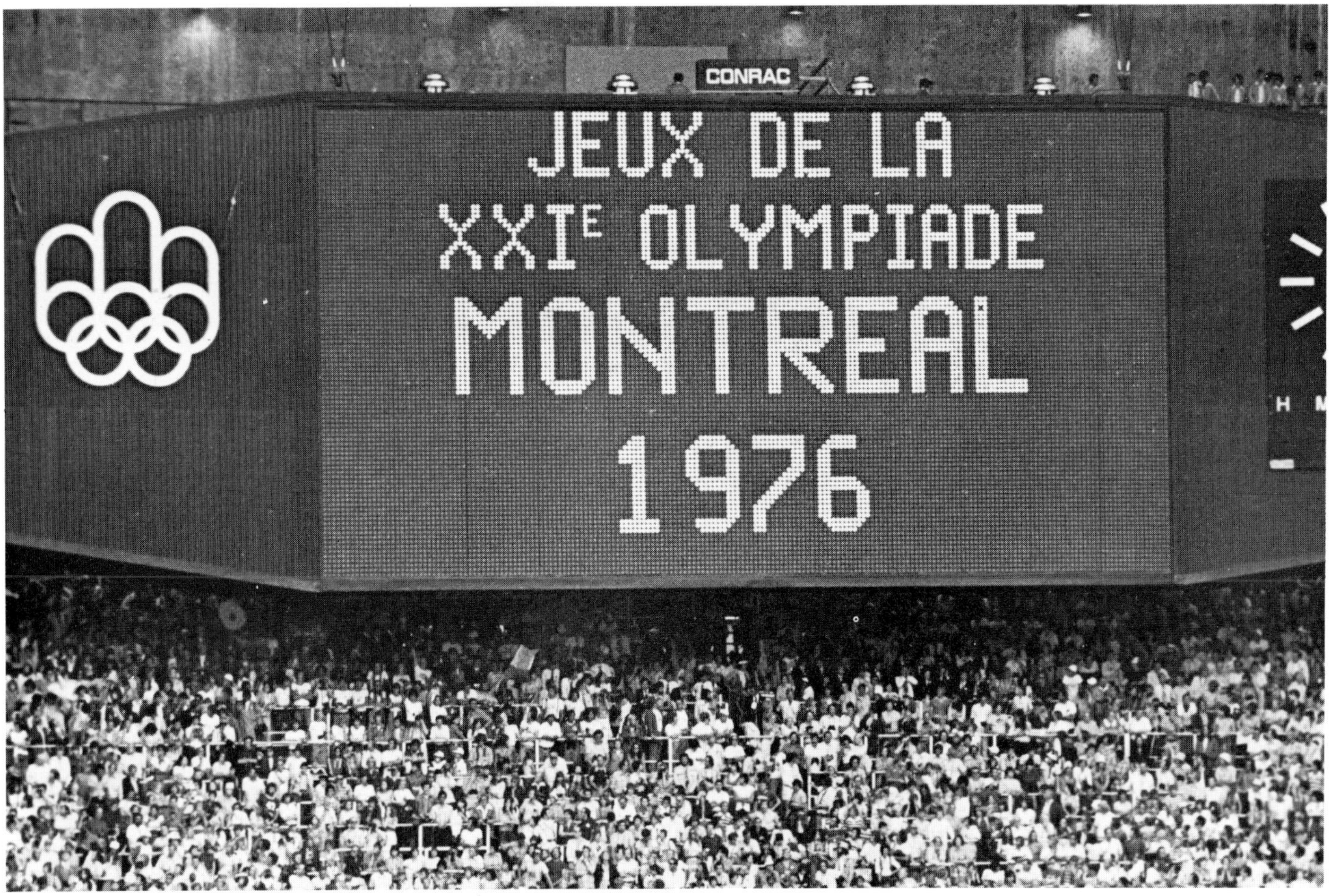
CONRAC
JEUX DE LA
XXIE OLYMPIADE
MONTREAL
1976

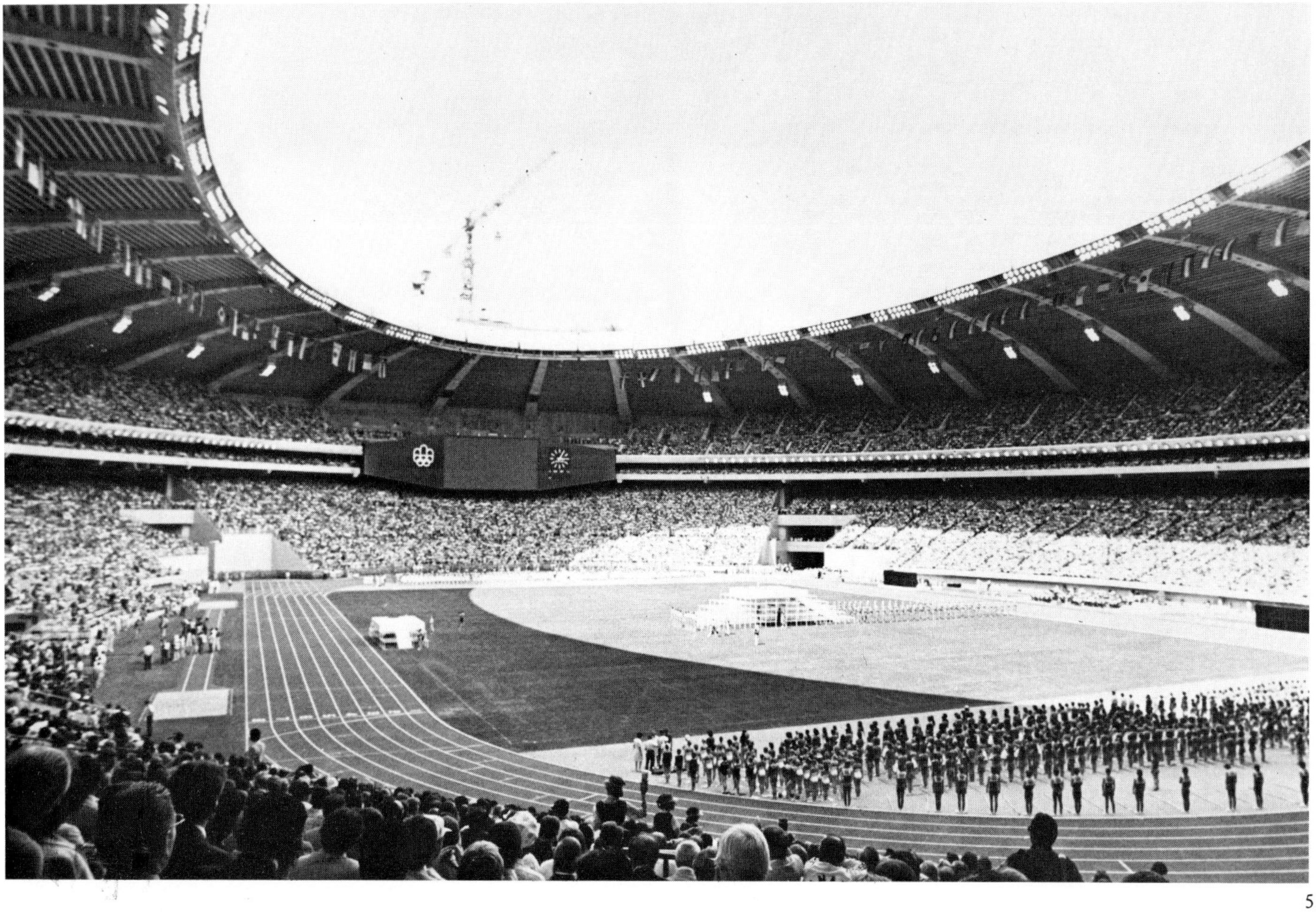

Don Quarrie leads Jamaica.

The USSR

Great Britain

—first win in that event for his country.

Then Hungarian Miklos Nemeth won his country's first gold in the javelin.

Then Don Quarrie took Jamaica's first-ever 200 gold.

Track's first half ended with Lasse Viren adding Finland to the rolls with a 10,000 victory.

The second half began in the same vein, as the USSR's Yuriy Syedikh annexed the hammer crown.

Then Guy Drut became the first Frenchman ever to win the 110 hurdles.

Then steepler Anders Garderud added Sweden's first gold since 1952.

Which meant that the first 13 gold medals had gone to 12 different nations, a remarkable spreading of the wealth.

There was little deviation from that point on, with John Walker's 1500 win adding only New Zealand to the list, although Juantorena's 400 win was the first for Cuba in that event, Jacek Wszola's high jump win was Poland's first-ever and Waldemar Cierpinski's marathon triumph was the first by a German. And one can wonder if the presence of the African nations might not have added another country or two to the ranks.

The women's side of the sport is undergoing radical changes also—in the other direction. The East Germans are now dominating there as the American

men used to (maybe even more so). In a shocking display of power at Montreal, they took nine of 14 golds, plus four silvers and six bronzes—for 19 of 38 medals available to them.

Why this curious dichotomy? Probably because the East Germans have invented a new sport, and are the finest practitioners of it. After a few years, after this new sport catches on everywhere, some balance will occur (until someone invents another one).

What new sport, you ask? Well, it is still called track and field of course; it's just how you prepare for it. The basics of the system, which filters all the talented people into special channels at young ages, also shows in the men's side, although not nearly as much. Add a liberal dash of sports medicine and a touch of the joys of being a respected athlete in a socialist country and you are ready.

Where the East Germans make it really different for their women is through the application of what many would call "men's training." Those sly devils. They

The Olympic Village, from the outside.

have discovered that women can run a lot of miles, do a lot of repetitions and lift a lot of weights. Their women don't come out of Wednesday afternoon gym class; they've been pointing towards the Olympic goal for years.

It is true that shot putters and discus throwers achieve a somatotype which would be considered "unfeminine" by Western standards, but the average East German athlete is just as appealing as the average American. (No matter what swimmer Shirley Babashoff says.)

Of course, one can recall when the Soviet Union burst on the scene in the early '50s. That nation's track fortunes quickly rose to a notable peak, then receded somewhat. The big breakthrough to total dominance never came. The East German star may already have reached supernova.

But no matter who the cast of characters includes, men or women, the true track fan can sit back and enjoy as the quest for the ultimate continues.

Here's hoping they never get there. □

The Olympic Village, from the inside.

Inside the Village—France's Guy Drut (l) and Jacques Rousseau confer with official and former mile great Michel Jazy.

The Olympic Stadium

—*Le Stade Olympique.*

Frank Shorter (US) marathon silver medalist.

Angela Voigt (East Germany) long jump champion.

Rosemarie Ackermann (East Germany) high jump champion.

Arnie Robinson (US) long jump champion.

July 17, 1976—

The Games of the XXI Olympiad begin.

Old Glory flew on the highest staff reserved for the winners, this time thanks to the men's 400 relay champions.

The winner's flag flew during the victory ceremonies—and for Lasse Viren after his 10,000 meter triumph. But guards kept his Finnish followers from the track after he won the 5000 meters *(opposite)*.

MIGHTY THROWERS—
Decathlon champion Bruce Jenner (US)
with a hair-raising shot put
(opposite). Miklos Nemeth (Hungary),
world record setting javelin winner *(left)*.
Ruth Fuchs (East Germany), women's javelin
champion for the second time *(below)*.

Arnie Robinson (US), men's long jump champion *(opposite)*.
Kathy McMillan (US), women's long jump silver medalist *(right)*.

The 1500 meter field strains to catch black-clad John Walker but to no avail.

Mac Wilkins (US), discus champion *(overleaf)*.

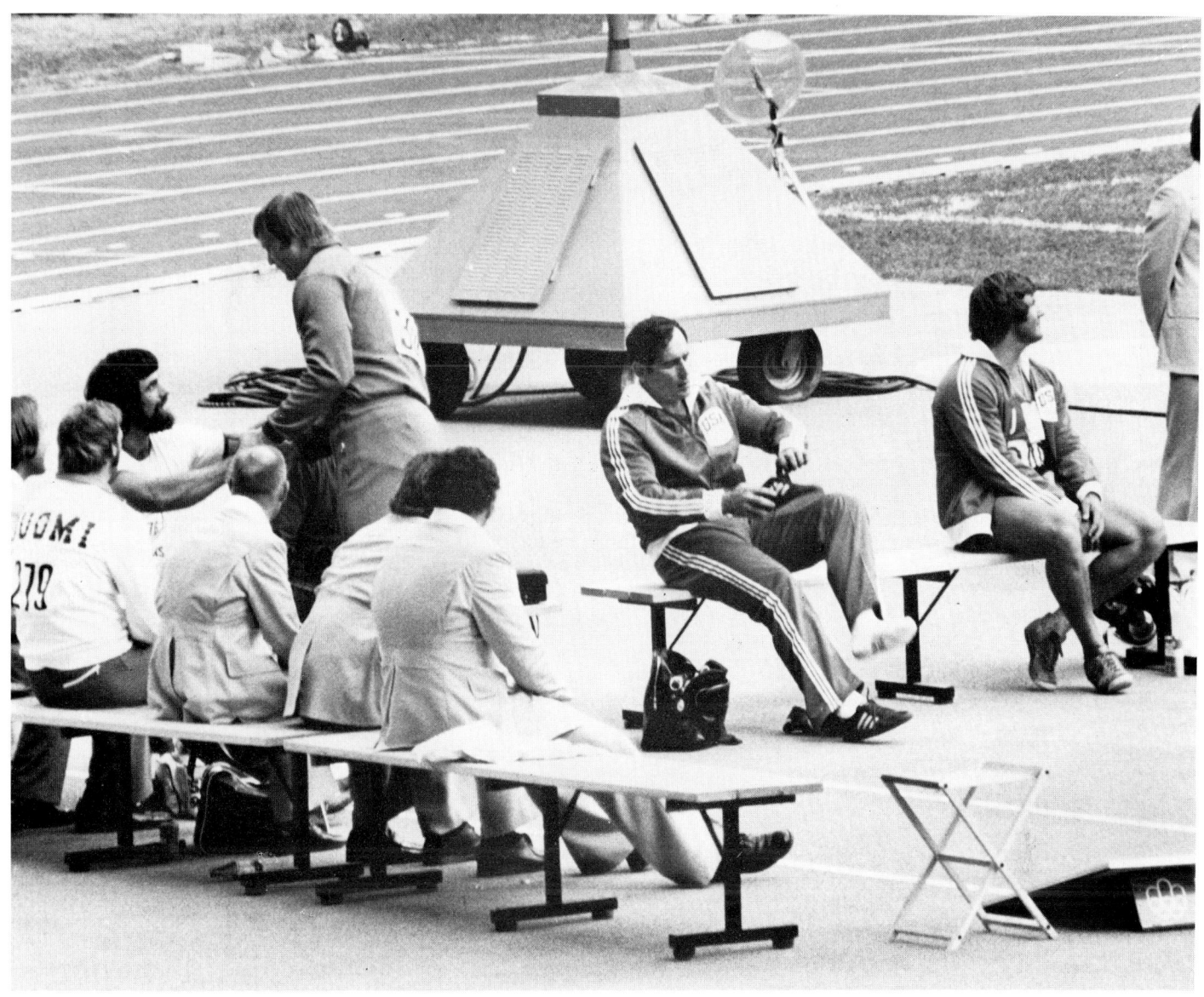

Discus champion Mac Wilkins (US) is congratulated by Siegfried Pachale (East Germany); Americans Jay Silvester and John Powell amuse themselves.

Annegret Richter (West Germany) 100 meter champion.

Chandra Cheeseborough (US) 100 meters.

Renate Stecher (East Germany) sprints.

Jan Merrill (US), Tatyana Kazankina (USSR), Gunhild Hoffmeister (East Germany), Nina Holmen (Finland) 1500 meter final.

Tatyana Kazankina (USSR) 800, 1500 meter champion.

Irena Szewinska (Poland) happy 400 meter champion.

Udo Beyer (East Germany) shot put champion.

Al Feuerbach (US) shot put.

Geoff Capes (Great Britain) shot put.

Dave Roberts (US) pole vault bronze medalist.

Americans Dave Roberts, Earl Bell and Terry Porter take a horizontal view of the vault.

Earl Bell (US) pole vault.

BEFORE THE FALL—Bronislaw Malinowski leads the steeplechase final with 1 lap to go from Frank Baumgartl, Anders Garderud and Tapio Kantanen.

... AND AFTER—Garderud is on his way to victory, Baumgartl is down off the last hurdle and Malinowski finds an unscheduled hurdle in his path.

Alberto Juantorena (Cuba) 400, 800 meter champion.

In a 1500 meter semi-final, left to right, Frank Clement, Paul-Heinz Wellmann, Rick Wohlhuter, Eamonn Coghlan, and Marc Nevens *(opposite)*.

John Walker (New Zealand) 1500 meter champion.

The United States' silver medal-winning 1600 meter relay team.

Debra Sapenter, Rosalyn Bryant, Pam Jiles.

Sheila Ingram, Sapenter, Bryant.

Jenner the King
by Bert Nelson

Were it not for the Olympics, the decathlon may very well be one of sportdom's least-rewarded activities. Indeed, except for the quadrennial Games—and despite them—the decathlete, when shorn of Olympic glamor, remains unknown, unrecognized, unappreciated and not in the least understood. Even among track fans, the event and the athletes receive little attention. And the rest of the sport's world is lucky if it can define the decathlon as a competition involving 10 events.

Come Olympic time, however, it is a different story. Far different.

From being low man on track's totem pole, the winning decathlete suddenly is hailed as "the world's greatest athlete." Or, at the least, "the greatest all-around athlete." And, so we are told by countless media people, he is the conqueror of a "grueling" competition.

So it was in Montreal. Athletes used to competing before "crowds" numbering in the low hundreds found themselves on stage before 75,000 live watchers. Plus tens of millions of television

The raised fist of victory became Jenner's trademark in Montreal.

viewers. And a press corps literally several times larger than the usual total attendance at a decathlon competition.

It was a time of mutual discovery. The decathloners were introduced to the heady bouquet of large-scale crowd appreciation. And the media, and through them the viewers, found a happening from which heroes are made. If not love at first sight, it was something akin to it.

The chief protagonists on the Montreal decathlon stage were Nikolay Avilov and Bruce Jenner. Avilov of the Soviet Union—tall, handsome, world record holder (automatic timing) and defending Olympic champion. Jenner of the United States—tall, handsome, world record holder (manual timing) and favored to become the new Olympic champion.

As the competition developed, Jenner quickly became the darling of the media and the viewers, American style. Aside from wearing USA on his broad chest, Jenner overshadowed his opponent in the charisma division. Avilov, outwardly unemotional

Determination in the 400...

...and then joy.

Defending champion Nikolay Avilov *(opposite)*.

and imperturbable, was no match here for the outgoing Jenner who responded with fervor to the crowd he knew was with him.

Then, as it became obvious Avilov was on this day also no match for his rival athletically, attention to Jenner swelled rapidly. Toward the end of the second day it was certain that Jenner not only would survive this grueling test of all-around athletic greatness, but would smash the world record in the process. When he did so with a pulsating finish—and an American flag was stuck in his hand, and he was joined by his photogenic wife—the making of a hero was complete.

The Olympic decathlon, which had produced the legendary Jim Thorpe and such latter-day supermen as Bob Mathias, Rafer Johnson and Bill Toomey, had once again cast in bronze an unforgettable image.

This time it was Bruce Jenner—superstar of the Montreal Olympics. □

Jenner leads other medalists Avilov (bronze) and Kratschmer (silver) in the 1500.

An ecstatic finish, congratulations from teammate Fred Samara and the fans love it.

THE KING IS DEAD; LONG LIVE THE KING—
Jenner succeeds Avilov as Olympic champion.

Joao Oliveira (Brazil) triple jump bronze medalist.

James Butts (US) triple jump silver medalist.

Alberto Juantorena (Cuba) celebrates his 800 meter victory.

Fred Newhouse (US) 400 meter silver medalist *(opposite)*.

Edwin Moses clears the last barrier of his world record 400 meter hurdles triumph ahead of US teammate Mike Shine (r).

Barbel Eckert (East Germany) wins the 200 meters ahead of 100 meter champion Annegret Richter (l).

Ron Laird, Larry Walker (US) 20-kilometer walk.

TAFNOT 76

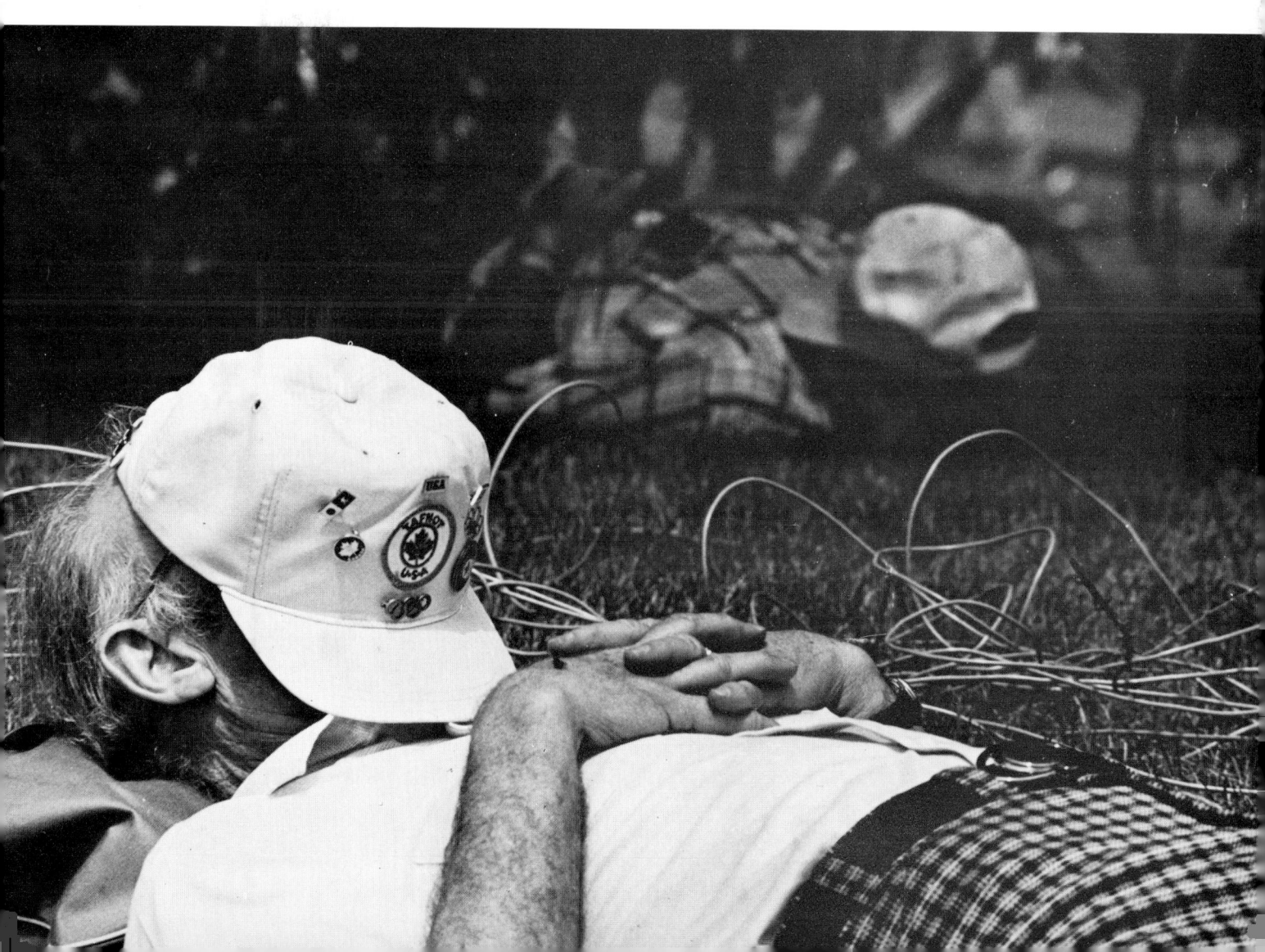

TAFNOT 76

An Olympic memories section of OLYMPIC IMAGES for members of TAFNOT 76, the Track & Field News Olympic Tour to Montreal

Again, our thanks to all of you who went to Montreal with T&FN those halcyon days of July (and a little bit of August) in the summer of '76. It was a trip to remember, with the thrilling track and field action the obvious highlight.

This portion of OLYMPIC IMAGES is our small attempt to recapture some of the features of our 1976 Olympic Tour and we hope it will bring back lots of fond memories for you: the gala party at the Place des Arts, the Hospitality Center at the Hotel Meridien, the stadium, the city, and above all, the people: TAFNOTers, staff members, the stadium and subway crowds, and the citizens of Montreal.

Our gratitude is due to several TAFNOTers for contributing to this memory section, particularly Don Chadez who was T&FN's official photographer at the Games. Fred and Jo Chez as usual snapped everything in sight in Montreal—giving us over 2,000 color prints to select from (sorry we couldn't have used more, Chezes!). Jim Terrill, now working full-time with Track & Field News, again has allowed us to share some of the whacky notions running through that peculiar brain. It's the third straight TAFNOT memory book to carry Jim's nutty cartoons.

And so, it's on to Moscow! Already, more than 2,000(!) have signed up for TAFNOT 80, a reflection of the incredible interest in the 1980 tour . . . and the confidence in TAFNOT. We are honestly flabbergasted. And 71 have signed already for 1984, eight for 1988, and two for 1992! Gee, wonder what color caps we'll have in '92...

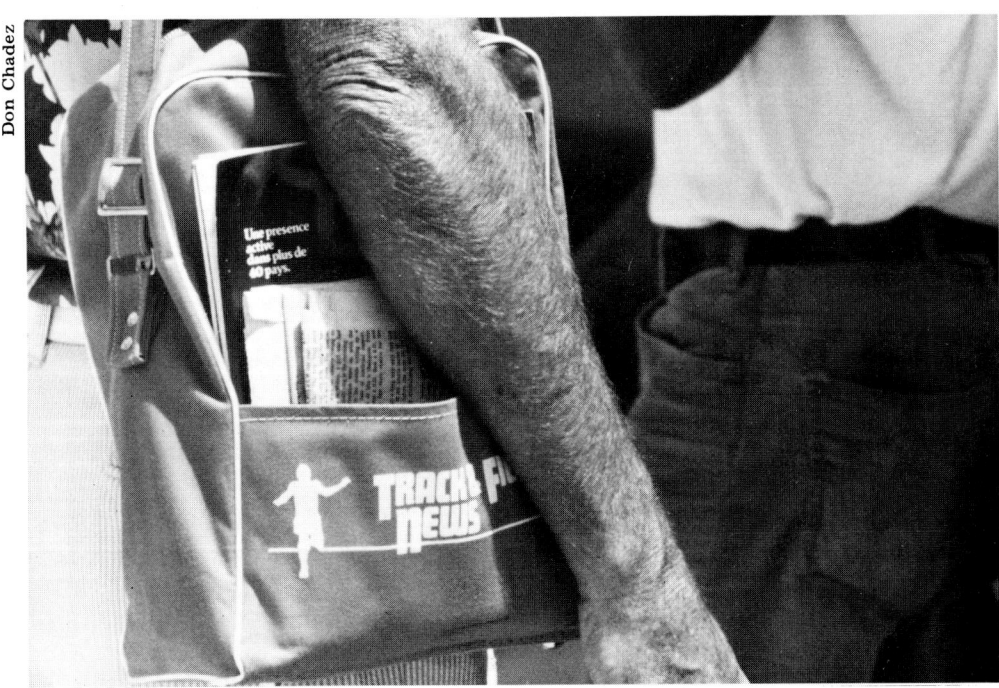

Photo at right by Don Chadez. TAFNOT 76 cover photo by Jim Engle.

EndGames

planes
zoomzoomzooom
below us treeshouseslakesmountainscarspeople
everything
clouds
we land
now there are people again
with all their baggage, packages, bundles
scattering home
to unpack them all
it is their *vacation*
and we are making it possible
soon
they are all over us,
asking, probing, inquiring
wherewhenhow??
will it get us there on time
do we have good seats
did you know our housing is cancelled?????
ah,
iced tea.........
it comes constantly
questions, and no answers
problems and no solutions
but in time, we solved most of them
they saw the Games
and had good seats
their housing housed them
and it was good
soon, there were no questions
dismantling
cleaning up
that was all that was left
there was silence
he sat alone, the office was silent
once there was everything
now
there is
nothing
gone are the GAMES
for a while at least

gone is me

patty schweikert

Patty Schweikert, who has worked in Track & Field News's main office in Los Altos, went to Montreal and was a TAFNOT 76 staff member. She now attends Foothill College in Los Altos Hills.

Photo above by Don Chadez; below, Bob Levie.

TAFNOT Veterans Roll of Honor

We'd like to salute those TAFNOT 76 members who've had the courage and endurance to make several Olympic trips with Track & Field News.

SEVEN OLYMPIC TOURS. Only three persons have been on all seven TAFNOT tours. Track & Field News founding editor Cordner Nelson and wife Mary, who now live in Carmel, California, and Jack Dozier of Stockton, California have the most TAFNOT service stripes. The Distinguished Travel Cross to all three!

SIX OLYMPIC TOURS. Another hardy group of four loyalists has attended six Olympic Games with TAFNOT: Bob Duddy of Reading, Pa., Bert Prichard of Onowa, Iowa, Uan Rasey of Studio City, California, and T&FN editor and publisher Bert Nelson.

FIVE OLYMPIC TOURS. Thirteen have gone to five Games with TAFNOT: Helen Prichard, Ruth Chartener, Walt Dabney, Syd DeRoner, Jim Gilbert, Myles and Blanche Grover, Nate Stinson, Paul Travis, Juan Zubillaga, Don Potts, and Irv and Gloria Alten.

FOUR OLYMPIC TOURS. Twenty-six TAFNOT 76ers have been to four Olympic Games with T&FN: Bill and Vivian Wright, Walt Murphy, David McGlone, Ralph Love, Merwin Seay, Bob Selfridge, Steve and Myrtle Chelbay, Ray and Betty Canton, Bob and Dorothy Decker, Dwight and Alberta Steele, Mel Dyche, Ray Kressler, Loren Sorensen, Ray and Betty Allington, Jim Barger, Richard Kirk, Dick Dodge, Ethel Carey, and Sam and Emily Monastero.

Only eight TAFNOT 76ers were with us for our very first excursion—to Helsinki in 1952: the three Nelsons, Jack Dozier, Uan Rasey, Bill and Vivian Wright, and Edgar McDowell.

1952	Helsinki, Finland	46 tour members
1956	Melbourne, Australia	69
1960	Rome, Italy	215
1964	Tokyo, Japan	176
1968	Mexico City, Mexico	817
1972	Munich, Germany	1100
1976	Montreal, Canada	2920
1980	Moscow, USSR	2142(!) (signed as of 11/1/76)

Seven-time TAFNOTer Cordner Nelson interviews U.S. men's team head track coach Leroy Walker at the TAFNOT party./Don Chadez photo.

TAFNOTers Scott McCullom, Elmer Lee, Leon and Jeffrey Washington, five-timer Paul Travis (kneeling), and George Bryan./Horace Wall photo.

U.S. team manager Bill Exum, Roberta and Marshall Romeo, and George Bryan./Horace Wall photo.

AT THE STADIUM

Photos by Fred Chez

TERRILLTOONS

THE HOSPITALITY CENTER

Where TAFNOTers got together for good conversation, refreshment, rest and recuperation, and TV viewing.

Photos by Don Chadez.

A9

Top: Some TAFNOTERS and TAFNOT staff at the stadium, including Gary Verigin, Dick Dodge, Tom Jordan, Garry Hill, Bob Pape, Bob Hersh, Linda and John Geer, and smilin' Ed Fox./ Nancy Hill photo.

Middle: What are these men happy about? Maybe it's those great seats in the press section . . . Bert Nelson, Garry Hill, and Don Steffens./Jon Hendershott photo.

Bottom: TAFNOT staffer Bertha Light has a way of getting cooperation from people. Here, a good Montreal gendarme cooperates in gag photo. Or is it a gag, Bertha?/Grace Light photo.

Letter from Janet Allen

There's probably little I can add to what's already been said about the excitement of seeing all those wonderful athletes in action. But I have other memories of the Olympics, too.

You Can't Change Your Image... But Who Wants To!

Being a native Berkeleyan and Cal Alum, I've become accustomed to being associated with the so-called rebel element. Still, I was surprised by the following events.

One afternoon I was watching gymnastics competition when Queen Elizabeth and her party entered and took their seats across the Forum from me. About five or ten minutes later, a man came walking down my row, stopped in front of my seat, and announced that he wished to search my bag (TAFNOT flight bag, of course). When he finished he spoke into his walkie-talkie, advising his partners that I was "clean." It would seem that the security officers had caught my visage in one of their large telescopes and felt I was worth checking out as a possible threat to the Queen. I must say, it made a good story to tell my family and friends, who know how harmless I really am.

Sports Experts

I was eating in a little restaurant in the Meridien Complexe when Track & Field News feature writer Jon Hendershott and some friends came in. Jon proved he's an expert in other sports besides track when he stopped in front of my table and advised me that the ball printed on my T-Shirt was a soccer ball. He was right; smart boy!

The qualifying round round for the men's High Jump was almost over when two men entered the section I was in and took the two seats next to me, which had just been vacated. They explained that their seats had been in another section, but they had come to this section to pick up their sons. One of them then asked me, "Is that fellow they've been booing supposed to be a good jumper or something?" When I explained that it was the world record holder, Dwight Stones, there was no glimmer of recognition in their eyes. What really blew my mind was that they were both wearing TAFNOT caps!

Celebrity Party

It was great being able to go home and tell my friends that I had spoken to Bruce Jenner and Dwight Stones. But I was also thoroughly charmed by some of the less well publicized athletes like the soft-spoken, friendly and good looking James Butts and Deby La Plante who would have won that TV set had it been awarded to the person with the greatest enthusiasm. Needless to say, I thoroughly enjoyed myself. I hope we'll be able to have a similar party in Moscow.

Janet Allen
Berkeley, Calif.

Left, Chrystie Jenner and Jon Hendershott. Right, the Complexe Desjardins, home of the TAFNOT Hospitality Center./Garry Hill photos.

THE HIGH COST OF MONTREAL

Everybody knows that these 1976 Olympics were by far the costliest in history. But no one knows just now costly. And perhaps they never will. The accounting may never be straightened out.

As the Games got underway the unofficial and undenied word was that the total cost had soared to more than $1,500,000,000. That's a billion and a half dollars. The impressive stadium had cost about $650,000,000. And it wasn't even finished. The tower, the roof, and everything else can be expected to cost another $100,000,000 or more.

Supposing the cost comes to $750 million. And supposing it was built with money borrowed at a cheap 6%, or that 6% is the value of the money forever tied up in the stadium complex. That's $45 million per year! And that's $123,000 for every day of the year. Montreal, or whoever ends up owning the stadium, will be lucky to see two or three percent of that.

Among other Olympic records is the Beamonesque "most money ever paid for a stadium". If you thought your ticket prices were high, take note that each seat in the stadium cost over $7500.

How did the Organizing Committee manage to spend that much money? It couldn't be easy. But *Sports Illustrated* gives a clue with a report on some of the fantastic waste in the Games:

The Olympic Village cost $85 million but can be sold as apartments for only $50 million. $1.5 million was spent on walkie-talkies. Three engineers were hired from a construction firm for nine months for $500,000. Thirty-three cranes were rented at a price that was $1 million more than it would have cost to buy them.

And the Montreal Symphony Orchestra and choirs that you saw at the closing ceremonies—they neither played nor sang a note. They merely pretended to make music (what you heard was recorded music), all in accordance with a musician's guild contract that forced the organizing committee to pay, whether or not the musicians were present, a fee of $500,000.

TAFNOT 76: Our Crying Towel

The Olympics cost the citizens of Montreal plenty, but they also cost our tour members and the TAFNOT organization a good deal too. Tickets ranged up to $50 per single event. Housing rates were two or even three times normal. Food and drink was expensive.

But there are some tour costs you may not know about. For instance, the Place des Arts

A view of the unfinished $750,000,000 stadium complex./Fred Chez photo.

charged, *in addition to its basic rental fee*, $827.89 for stagehands. And what did they do? Literally no more than install two microphones, a table and three chairs and stairs to the stage, plus lowering the curtain and providing one spotlight operator.

Printing costs of the TAFNOT Press were several times higher than they should have been or would have been in Los Altos which, as part of the metropolitan San Francisco area, suffers from the third highest cost of living in the US. A single sheet, 2300 copies, cost $250. Then the government collected a 20% tax! The bill was $313. Unless the Press was printed on a weekend in which case the cost could go as high as $433 with labor at time-and-a-half. Total printing costs were $4861.08.

And then there was the Meridien Hotel: Item: Television sets rented to us at $20 per day each. For 17 days that is $340 or about what the sets cost the Meridien wholesale.

Item: Coffee at $8.50 a gallon plus 8% tax which came to $.57 per 8 oz. cup of coffee. And they didn't provide any service.

Item: Soft drinks at $.50 each plus 15% service (for what?) plus 8% tax for a total of $.62 each.

Item: Food and drink at the Celebrity Party at the Place des Arts, catered by the Meridien. Canapes, which were mediocre at best, for $6750. Fruit punch, also mediocre, $5000! Plus 15% service. Plus 8% tax. Total cost for the canapes and punch, $14,452.50.

Note, too, that these prices are in Canadian dollars which means they were about 3% higher in US dollars.

So why did we pay these exorbitant charges? Simple enough. We had to. The hotel wouldn't let us bring in our own rented TVs, or buy coffee or soft drinks from another source. Or give us a better rate on the canapes and punch. (Actually they wanted to charge more on the punch but eventually came down a bit.) So it was pay their price or forego the items.

Hotel banquet costs always are ridiculous when compared with comparable food and service elsewhere. And of course the Meridien, like almost everyone else in Montreal, took advantage of the opportunity.

The breakfasts and lunches at the Hospitality Center cost $6.67 each, including tax (8%) and service (15%). Again, the same food elsewhere would be

Starring, at far left, some of that $5000 fruit punch!

considerably less. But this is about par for first class hotels. And it was mandatory to buy the meals in order to have the excellent facilities of the Hospitality Center. No kick there.

One final note. The free coffee cost $4417.02 and the free soft drinks $3782.70. These were extras, not advertised as part of the Olympic tour, and were gladly provided until we realized how fast the bill was running up and, on top of very high and unexpected extra housing costs, began to wonder where the money was coming from.

The Complexe Desjardins./Don Chadez photo.

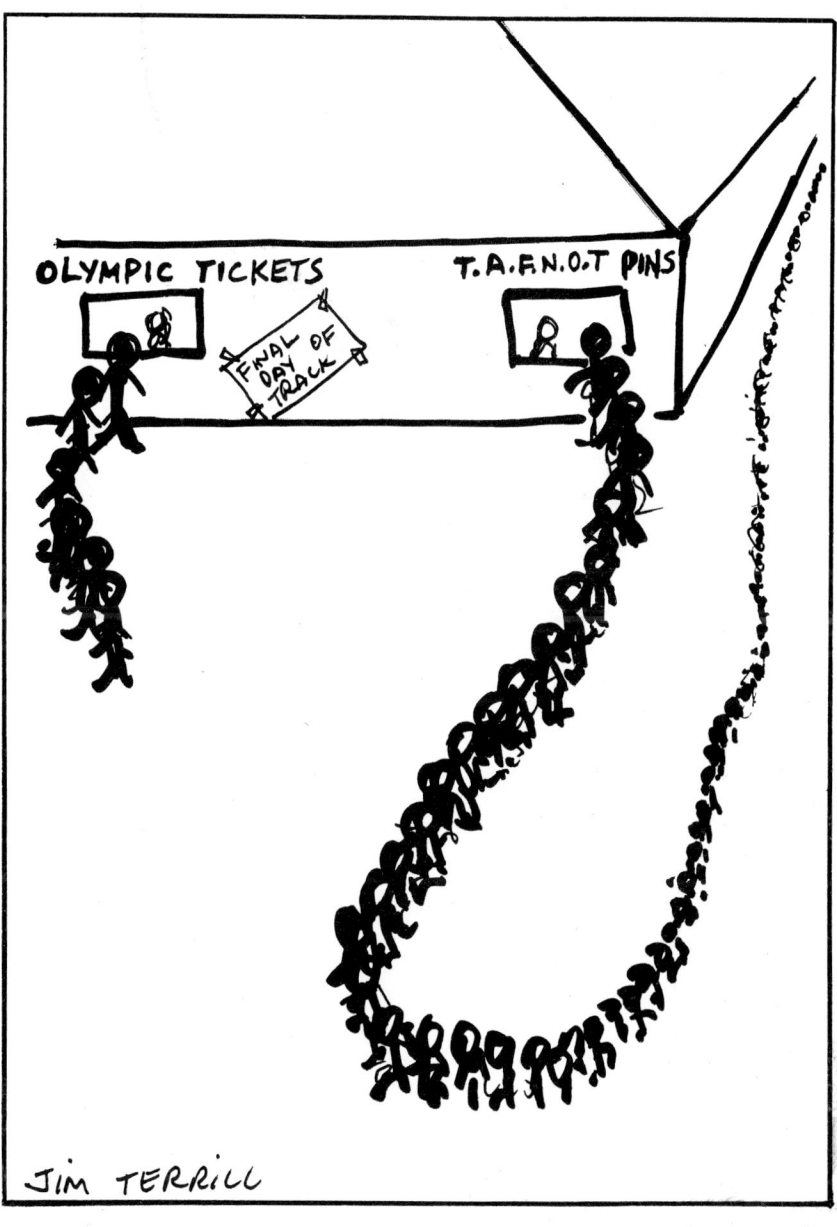

For pin collectors only.

Photo above, Bob Levie.
Above right, Don Chadez.

THE PARTY

Photos by Don Chadez

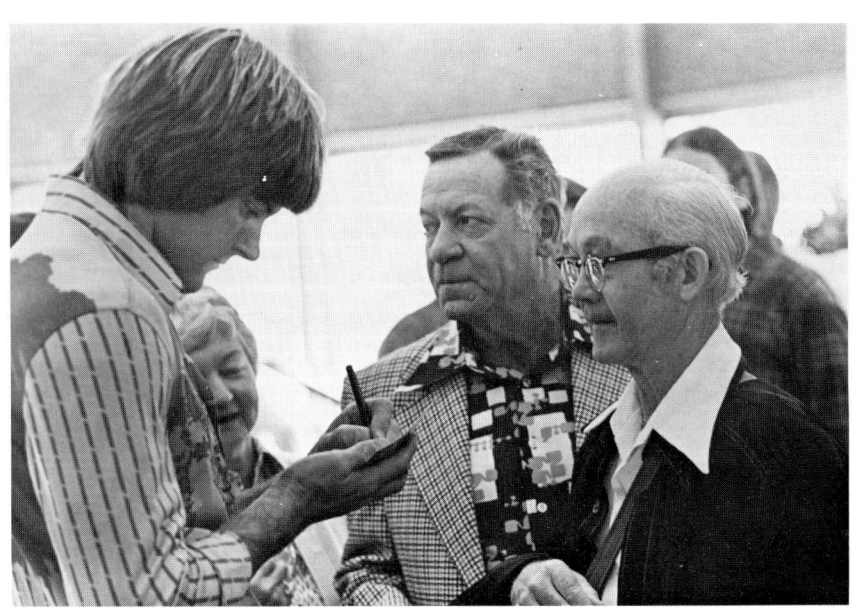

Above left, the inimitable Tom Ecker "warms up" the crowd. Above right, Alex Ferenczy and Evie Dennis, U.S. women's track and field team head coach and manager, talk to Frank Litsky of the New York Times. Right, Bruce Jenner signs autographs for TAFNOTers.

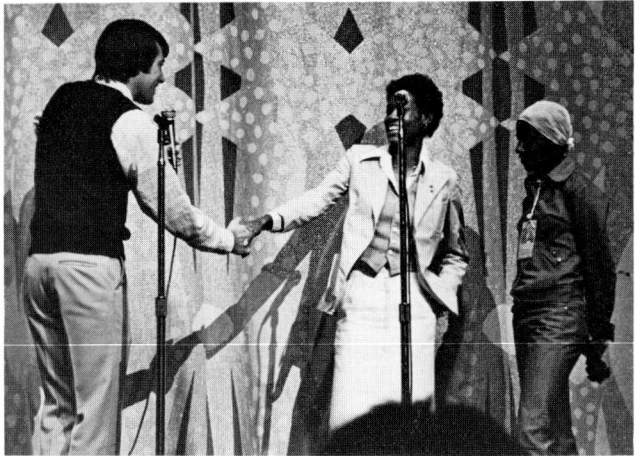

Above, Bert Nelson and Lee Evans. Right, from top to bottom, Garry Hill and Dwight Stones; Tom Jordan, Debra Sapenter and Sheila Ingram; Edwin Moses and Jon Hendershott; Bert Nelson and Bruce Jenner./Don Chadez photos.

A19

Photos on A19 and A20 by Don Chadez.

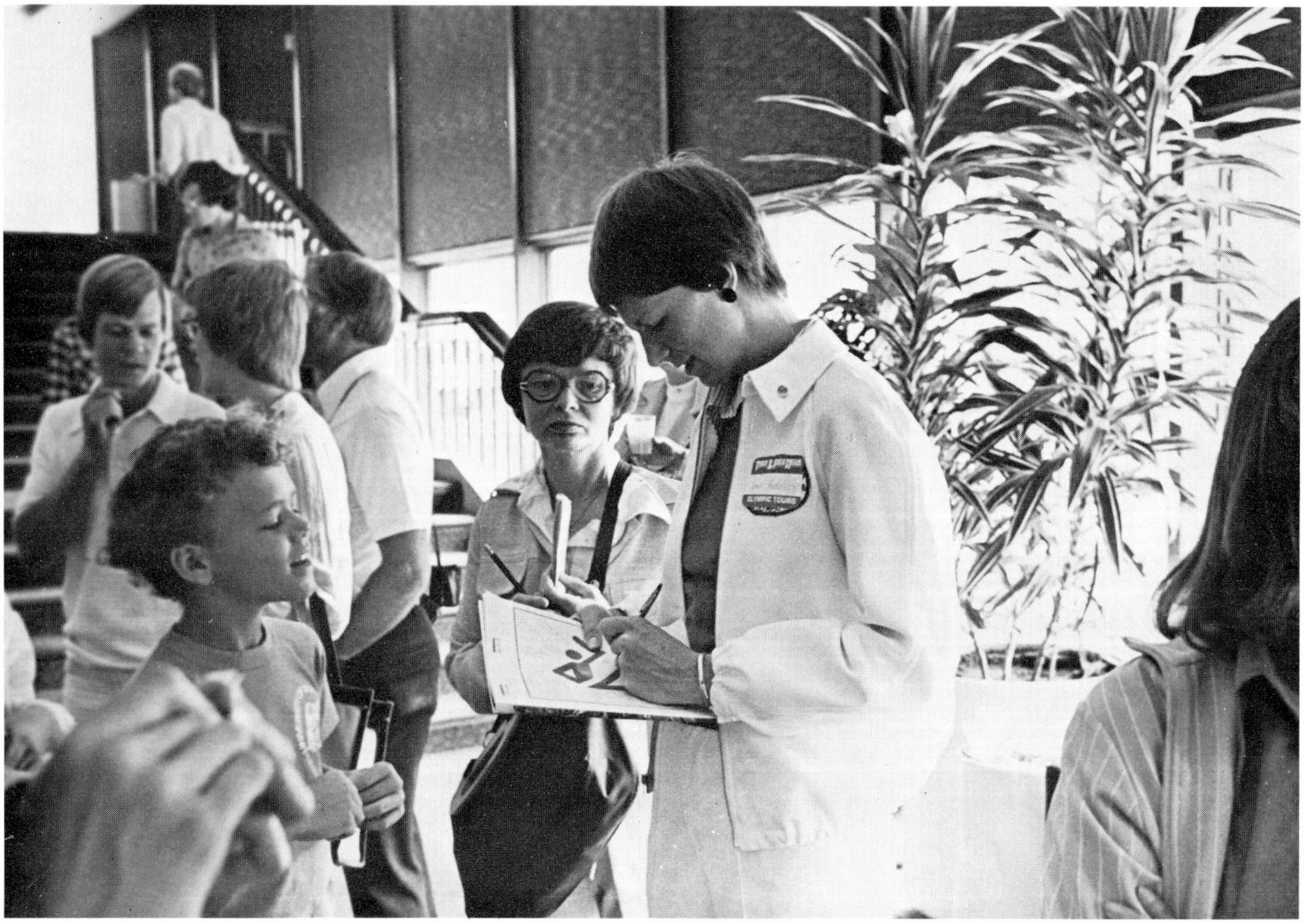

QUESTIONNAIRE RESPONSE

The good, the bad and the ugly

Results of the TAFNOT 76 Survey are a rather pleasant surprise. We felt very certain the tour was a success. But we weren't prepared for the degree of success accorded TAFNOT by your ballots.

There were reasons, certainly, for some to judge the tour as less than outstanding. The housing situation wasn't good for many people. And the stadium was poorly constructed for track. And prices were up. The bus strike didn't help. Etc. So we anticipated some sincere displeasure, or at least disappointment, even though most of the disturbing elements were not under our control.

And it is hard for us to produce a balanced judgment. Those of us on the firing line, dealing with cancelled or substandard housing problems, for instance, could be forgiven for feeling everyone on the tour was unhappy. Those of us out front, talking track, meeting old friends and making new ones, sharing the joy of the Olympics, receiving unsolicited compliments, could just as easily feel everyone was tremendously pleased.

Realization that only a small portion of the tour had big problems, and that we had helped to solve most of the problems, aided us in assessing the tour overall. And when we got home and began to receive letters, notes and phone comments and the 1980 deposits poured in, we knew we had a hit on our hands. Even so, the degree of acceptance was a bit surprising.

HOW DO YOU RATE THE TOUR OVER-ALL?

Super fantastic	18.5%
Excellent	62.1%
Good	17.3%
Fair	1.6%
Lousy	.5%

That's 97.9% rating the tour good or better. And 80.6% rating it excellent or better. We don't see how the ratings could be any better, remembering that you can't please everyone every time. We're sorry about the very few who had a lousy tour, or even just a fair one. We would like everyone to have a tour that was at least good. And we will continue to work for it, just as we did after Munich when the survey results were: Super fantastic 11.1%; excellent 62.7%; good 21.7%; fair 3.5%; lousy 1.1%. Good or better 95.5%; excellent or better 73.8%. No surveys were taken on the 1952-68 tours.

THE WHYS AND WHEREFORES OF THE SURVEY

The survey is taken for several reasons. We want to know what we did right and wrong so that we can do more of the former and less of the latter on the next tour. Aside from the fact that it's good business to get customer reaction we are very anxious to please. We have a lot of good friends on the tour, and people who put their Olympic plans in our hands in good faith, and the reputation of our magazine is at stake. So we do try hard and the survey helps grade our effort. Thirdly, we pick up some good ideas, big and small, for future tours. Finally, we've found that you enjoy reading the comments of others, sharing and comparing experiences and reactions.

THANKS

Thanks for responding to the survey and for passing on your comments and constructive criticism. We don't always agree, but we're still glad to have even the comments we considered unjustified. It all helps.

And thanks especially for your patience and understanding. If you didn't understand that the over-sold Olympics creates a shortage and over-pricing of everything, and that some factors were beyond our control, you would be justified in rendering a different judgment. Housing, of course, was the major problem. 35% rated it either fair (27%) or awful (8%). Yet only 2.1% rated the overall tour either fair or lousy. The acceptance of poor housing without letting it spoil the tour and the Games reveals a mature understanding of the problems involved. And it does take understanding and a love for the Games because where and how you live is a major consideration. Surprisingly, there were several who felt their housing was downright "awful" yet rated the tour "super fantastic".

THE DETAILED RESULTS

Answers to each of the questions will be accompanied by comments. Where we feel a comment on your comment is appropriate it will appear in parentheses immediately following the tour member's comment. Names will not be used but all material will remain on file in case anyone wants to check it.

No attempt will be made to present a totally balanced picture. There will be far more negative comments proportionately than the overall rating of the tour would call for. Since the good far outweighs the bad it would be repetitious to repeat the nice things over and over. And it wouldn't be very useful. Still, we will pass along a lot of the nice reaction. It's an interesting form of personal expression and it, too, can be useful.

GENERAL REACTION

Results are noted above. Comments follow.

The tour was absolutely superb and the staff deserves a great deal of credit for taking care of all the details.

I had meant to write you just as soon as I got home, but I just had to tell everyone what a fantastic time I had. Felt really at home during the entire stay. Really hated to pack it up and head back to the real world. The best vacation I've ever had.

Thank you for a good time.

Olympics themselves were great. Housing was poor and way overpriced. Didn't like the inclusion of extras I didn't want or use—pins, hat, bag, etc.—which made tour too expensive.

Overall a very enjoyable trip. We were very pleased and impressed with your ability to assign seats and housing with our friends.

The tour was great. I sympathize with the planners of the tours over the incredible hassles that the Montreal Olympics incurred. (Thanks. We don't really need or want sympathy, but your understanding of the obstacles helps.)

This was our fifth trip with Track & Field News. We've never been disappointed. We intend to make at least one trip a year with you, wherever you are going. Rudy, Ed and everyone do a super job for us every time. Count on us for a testimonial anytime you need it. (Next time is the World Cup in Dusseldorf, Germany, in 1977, followed by the Commonwealth Games in Edmonton, Canada, 1978.)

It's so nice to hear from you, via the bulletin. It was an awful letdown after Montreal not to be hearing from you every once in a while!

Thanks for a helluva fine tour—considering the conditions you had to contend with at Montreal.

Don't take yourselves so seriously. (Frankly, we don't understand this comment. But it is a serious business trying to give 2920 trusting customers their money's worth.)

Don't take my remarks to be too negative. If they were I would not have already signed up for the 1980 and 1984 tours.

Lousy operation. Unfair treatment of tour members.

Thank you all once more. We really appreciated your efforts. We signed into your group very late, probably one of the last, after being disappointed by another group. We had all but given up hope when you came to our rescue and we certainly did enjoy, not only the Olympics and Montreal, but our assiciation with you. Needless to say we will never again attend any Olympic Games unless we go with TAFNOT.

I'd like to thank the TAFNOT staff for 17 memorable days!

Great tour. I won't miss another Olympics!

To express myself adequately I would include all the good comments listed in the '80 brochure. I, too, would use words like gentlemen, friendly, cordial, and efficient to describe your people ... and words like superb, perfect, fantastic and super to describe the overall tour. Thanks, and I vow I'll be back!

Very good tour. I know and expect this from you. On your tours since 1968. Going to Moscow, too.

TRACK TICKETS

Great 31%; good 51%; fair 14%; awful 4%. Comments:

Ticket prices were outrageous. (Perhaps. And it probably will get worse before it gets better. As long as the world stands in line to buy the tickets, no hard-pressed organizing committee is going to sell them for less than the traffic will bear. That's one reason we'd like to see the Games split and divided among several cities.)

Tickets were only fair, but were as good or better than can realistically be expected.

We would be happy to pay more for better seats to track. Maybe you should offer an option on this. (It wouldn't do any good. Price was not the criterion. Many higher priced seats were not as good as lower priced seats. The stadium seating plan was ridiculous, highlighted by Class I seats just a few feet away from class V seats, for instance. And furthermore, no seating map, with row numbers, etc. was obtainable before the Games.)

We requested track tickets next to our friends and they

weren't. (We apologize. It was our intent to do so and in virtually all cases we did, including yours for several days. But somebody goofed.)

Do not change tickets without asking the buyers permission. (Sorry, that is impractical. Tickets sold out in a hurry and if we had taken time to ask you if you would accept another price ticket they would have been gone. As you know, a lot of tickets were unavailable as it was.) Don't buy tickets behind TV monitors and cameramen. (We wouldn't, intentionally. But when the tickets are purchased neither the location of the seats nor the plans of the TV are known. It's a case of bad luck.)

Would have appreciated not being with the same group every day. Would have enjoyed an opportunity to meet more of the tour members.

I liked the way you sat beside the same people every day so you could rehash yesterday's events. I thank TAFNOT for the hard work it took to provide me with this fringe benefit.

We were about number 2100 to sign up and we sat beside a fellow who was no. 80 to sign up. I am wondering how the priority system works in relation to when you sign because I feel he definitely should have had better seats than myself. (First, we would like everyone to have the *same* quality seats, housing, etc., regardless of priority. But when there is a shortage of some tour element we feel priority of reservation is the fairest method of allocation. Priority was a prime concern in allocating housing but not with tickets. Everyone got the same dollar value worth of tickets. The mix of the various categories of tickets totaled the same, within $1. If you had more class IV tickets than somebody else, you probably had more class I and II tickets also. So in theory, at least, everyone had the same quality of tickets. Sometimes, of course, the luck of the draw made a higher priced ticket less good, and with certain events in the corners of the stadium a seat may be poor one day but excellent for another day's events.)

Track seats would have been excellent if the stadium had been designed for track events, no doubt! (True. Unfortunately we couldn't help that.)

Ticket positions could have been better, however, if someone had actually sat in the seats beforehand. Such is life. (If this means the stadium designer should have sat in the seats we must agree. If it means TAFNOT should have sat in the seats we must explain the impossibility. First, there was no choice of tickets. Second, even if there had been it wouldn't have done any good. Even the ticket manager of the entire Olympics didn't have a detailed seating chart until well after we had distributed our tickets. The organizing committee sent tickets all over the world and the national agents distributed them, all without knowledge of where each ticket was located!)

We paid good prices for tickets and sat in seats third row from the top. Some of the people had $18 tickets and they sat rows below us. We had $24 tickets. (Sorry but true. So isn't it a good thing that we didn't offer the option of paying more for tickets? What a blow it would have been to have bought all top price tickets and find all of them less good than lower priced tickets.)

We had bum tickets twice. That couldn't be helped. We're with you.

Stadium, first class! Let's forget the invisible corners of the track and long and triple jump pits. I sat only a few feet away from both and couldn't see them jumping but watched the instant replay on the scoreboard. But the seats were comfortable and that is so important for a 12 hour day.

It seemed as though, in comparison with other

The Olympic Village./Don Chadez photo.

TAFNOTers, I had a disproportionately large percentage of track seats in the top stadium sections. (Perhaps. But the dollar value was the same. And when the tickets left our office there literally was no way of knowing whether tickets were high or low.)

Seat prices often had nothing to do with quality of view.

Thought too many track tickets were poor for the price.

Problems were in stadium being for soccer, not track. (Actually, for professional baseball and football.)

Tickets generally were good. The worst set cost the most, $24. I sat by the scoreboard and could not see the opposite board or any part of the track run on the curve.

Whenever I felt like complaining about my tickets I looked at the standing room section and felt better. (It is good to remember that a lot of people couldn't buy seats, or even standing room. And 14,000 people had to stand each day. One tour, by another magazine, had about half standing tickets.)

Our tickets were fair but it wasn't your fault.

HOUSING

Great 26%; good 39%; fair 27%; awful 8%. Comments:

Housing was good except for the bus strike and roommate, who was a heavy smoker. (We couldn't anticipate the bus strike or do anything about it. We tried to keep smokers away from non-smokers. But not every smoker would admit it on the questionnaire. And some housing situations were so difficult that we had no choice but to mix the two.)

Under the circumstances, hard to beat.

We were among the first 50 to sign up yet we were located 41 miles north of the city. No excuse for this. (Actually, you were No. 1578 to sign up, in the lower half. And you indicated you wanted a public, commercial accommodation at about $10 a night. You had a car. We found a hotel in your price range despite your low priority.)

Arranged housing fell through and we got housing ourselves but you were prompt and efficient about the refund. (That was one of the biggest problems. Confirmed, official housing from the housing bureau, paid in advance, suddenly was cancelled. A very bad problem that took a lot of work and money on our part, a lot of understanding and patience on yours.)

Cost of housing not comparable to quality. (All too true, as we recognized all along in the tour bulletins.)

You should try to let people know where they will stay before arriving. (We did, with the few exceptions of those whose homes were cancelled too late to make a replacement.)

You may have been a little slow in paying my hosts. (The HEQUO procedure is for them to be paid after your visit. We paid in full before your visit, the money was held in bond, to be paid upon presentation of the housing voucher.)

Everything OK except for housing. It would have been less expensive at a good central hotel and would not have cost three hours a day commuting. (True enough. But there were no good central hotels with space beforehand. Your motel was excellent when we inspected it, and there was special Olympic transportation. But then came the bus strike.)

De Province Hotel was poor for the price but the location was great.

Our stay at the De Province at $40 per night was robbery. Someone didn't do their homework. (The hotel was inspected and was described as an old, second class hotel, well located and overpriced along with everything else in Montreal.)

The De Province was nice and the location was great.

If I ask for certain housing at a certain price tell me in advance what it's like, if possible. (We tried. Descriptions went with all commercial housing assignments. But it couldn't be done with each private room.)

We would like deluxe accommodations. TAFNOT should attempt to obtain a percentage of best accommodations to satisfy those of us who want them. (Where have you been? We reported many times that no deluxe accommodations were available, or even first class. We tried over and over again.)

Our housing wasn't too close, yet our hosts were the nicest people we could have had.

The hotel was run by the gay liberation movement. Couldn't even sit in the lobby without having the gay front all over the place.

Housing was good but overpriced at least three times. (Wouldn't doubt it. We hope you know you paid us exactly what we paid the landlord. There was no mark-up on housing.)

Our room was almost impossible. I would suggest that somehow you convey what accommodation one is really getting for a given price. (We tried, but it is difficult as each has his own standards. Note above that some thought the De Province was nice and others thought it robbery.)

Housing left quite a bit to be desired. Prices were at least doubled and maybe more. However, T&FN has covered all this

and your organization was appalled by the lack of housing organization and greediness.

Our rented basement flat was really primitive and the cost exorbitant. I suspect you won't have that kind of problem in Moscow. Probably won't be any flats to rent.

TAFNOT made a mistake in not checking to be sure that housing rate hikes were made for improvements actually provided. (HEQUO supposedly did this. They were to inspect and rate every home and set the prices. Even if we had inspected every home there was nothing we could do to change the price.)

Housing price was high but it wasn't your fault.

Did not use TAFNOT housing and my own arrangement was poor.

De Province was bad. I wouldn't stay there ordinarily but during the Olympics it was cheap and close to the Metro. I was better off than some.

On arrival we were informed our private residence had been cancelled. A call to TAFNOT headquarters and 15 minutes after our arrival we were on our way to our new home. We have blessed the day the original cancelled as the new home was much nicer and many times closer to the stadium.

Our private home was superior and it was astonishing to me that a family who lived as this family did would consider renting their apartment.

Housing was fair but was in accordance with our request and price range. (Price should be kept in mind. Many tour members asked for housing at $6 or $8 per night. Some then complained because they did not have high quality housing.)

You need to do everything possible to insure adequate housing. (Right you are. As you know from our many bulletin accounts, it is a most difficult problem and we do everything we can. We are no more happy about the housing situation than you are and can take solace only in the fact that most people were in the same situation and many were worse off.)

Our camping ground was the worst place we have ever found, bar none. I have to admit that it received four stars in Woodall Camp directory and that I cannot understand. It wasn't your fault.

The first morning my kind host insisted on taking me on bus and subway all the way to the stadium. (Many tour members report their hosts were wonderful and very helpful. A few report the opposite.)

Was willing to pay more for lodging to get what I'm accustomed to. The price was right but the quality wasn't middle class by U.S. standards. (That was a problem. We described the price range as HEQUO described it. But that price didn't buy what you or we are accustomed to for those dollars.)

MORE GENERAL REACTION

We felt that TAFNOT did a fine job but that Montreal was conducting a rip-off of the Olympic visitors.

It was everything you promised.

Most enjoyed the good companionship and track talk of the people we were seated with.

TAFNOT 76 was equal to TAFNOT 68 which was the best two weeks of my life. You get the idea. Thanks.

I didn't rate it super fantastic. Nothing is that good.

Thanks for showing the real Olympics, not the ABC Olympics.

Very enjoyable experience. Most interesting and rewarding part was the stay in a private home.

TAFNOT saved us a lot of headaches that individuals on other tours had. I'm definitely going in 1980.

Considering everything, you people have an "impossible" task and you do a fantastic job getting it accomplished and trying to satisfy everyone.

This was to be my first and last tour, but I'm hooked.

A great experience. Friendly atmosphere everywhere much appreciated. A lifetime goal achieved with wonderful memories to treasure.

I was treated like a king in Montreal.

Too many track nuts for me, but that's personal bias.

Stadium biggest disappointment. No coffee. And that business with the programs. But your end was superb.

Pleasantly surprised that you were able to handle almost 3000 people so well.

HOSPITALITY CENTER

Great 64%; good 33%; fair 3%. Comments:

Absolutely fantastic.

Most attractive part of the tour.

A life-saver for those staying out of town.

If you were not staying close to the hospitality center it was difficult and expensive to take advantage of it. (For some the opposite was true. See above.)

Unless you got to go to the hospitality center you felt left out. (It was there for you to enjoy. Your choice.)

The most important and significant thing you did was to establish the H.C. What a great idea and judging from its usage we weren't the only ones who thought so. For us it was a

Who says TAFNOT doesn't seat people together at the stadium?/Bob Levie photo.

chance to get out of our 11x13 hotel cell, which provided us with a place to sleep.

Free drinks were supposed to be part of the tour package. Why was it discontinued after a couple of days? (It was not supposed to be part of the tour package. Was never advertised as such. We had some money in our contingency budget and when it looked as if we wouldn't need it decided to offer free drinks. It went on for much longer than a couple of days but when the bills piled up—see article on high cost of Montreal—and we found ourselves paying double for some housing it was necessary to discontinue it.)

I could do without the H.C.

Great. Super fantastic. More than one could want.

I didn't get my free coffee one day. What's the matter with you guys. (That's life, we guess. Give something unexpected for free and get no thanks. Stop giving and you get blasted.)

The best idea yet. Many, many thanks.

PROGRAMS AT HOSPITALITY CENTER

Great 54%; good 42%; fair 4%. Comments:

Programs were tops and possibly one of the things that will be remembered longer than anything else.

Really enjoyed the luncheons and guests.

I don't know about the programs. You never did anything while I was there.

Loved the track talk sessions and everybody we met.

Particularly enjoyed Cordner, Bert and Garry in bull sessions.

Almost impossible for me to miss it at any Olympic Games in the future because of the information you give at the H.C. (The track talk sessions were so well received that we're planning more at all future tours, Olympic and otherwise. It's a great chance for us to share thoughts and opinions with you.)

CELEBRITY PARTY

Great 55%; good 38%; fair 7%; awful .1%. Comments:
Most worthwhile event. Don't drop for any reason.

Almost missed it because the description in bulletins sound as if it would be a dull cocktail party when in fact it was great. (Sorry, but we can't locate any such description. Glad you made it.)

Prefer night party. (You can't get the athletes until the Games are over and the night of Aug. 1 would have conflicted with closing ceremonies.)

Prefer dinner if possible. (Impossible. No place big enough. Besides, it doesn't work too well. Serving and eating interferes with program. We can eat anywhere in the world but this is a rare opportunity to listen to the competitors first hand.)

We were unable to attend as we made arrangements in accordance with information it would be Saturday night. Felt we missed out on an important part of the tour. (You did, and we're sorry.)

I suggest more "socializing" time with athletes at party. There were too many and too little time. (It would be nice but of course we can't require the athletes to stand around and talk with us. We are grateful they took the time to participate in the program.)

Hope future parties can be held the last night of track. We missed it because we took an early plane out. (The last night

Don Chadez

of track is difficult and risky because athletes aren't always available. This time there was no choice as we couldn't get the Place des Arts until the Organizing Committee finished with it July 31 and there was no place else in town that could handle us. Also, the last night of track had several finals in other sports many people wanted to see.)

Had a ticket and couldn't be in two places at one time.

No need for hors d'oeuvres. (You're right. Thought it would be a nice touch. But the price was a rip-off and service poor. Let's stick with the program.)

Loved the Celebrity Party. Glad you held it at the Place des Arts. The name sort of typifies the sport.

Don't call it a celebrity party. It's not. A press conference. A period of hero worshipping for some of your reporters, but not a celebrity party. (A rather strange comment from the *lone* tour member to rate the CP "awful.")

Party outside the auditorium needed at least two knowledgeable hosts or hostesses to help out. I only accidentally bumped into athletes or vice versa. (We had about 15 hosts/hostesses. But with some 2500 tour members and 50 athletes, arriving at different times, there isn't much that can be done to be sure you and the athletes get togerther.)

TOUR MANAGEMENT

Great 56%; good 39%; fair 4%; awful .75%. Comments:
Staff most pleasant and helpful.
Probably most concerned and helpful I've ever seen.
Great, considering all the hang-ups.
I was especially impressed by staff's ability to treat one with individual concern despite the enormous responsibility and work load.
TAFNOT personnel was extremely helpful when our assigned housing turned out to be lousy. We got new lodging immediately.
Great, except for travel.
Found all of your people to be extremely friendly and helpful. A far cry from what I heard concerning other groups.
Great.

PLANNING

Great 59%; good 35%; fair 5%; awful .75%. Comments:
Excellent planning, don't know how you did it so well.
Fantastic for that number of people.
Super fantastic.
The planning and executing of the Montreal tour must rank with Hannibal's march over the Alps. Frankly, I don't know how you did it.

TICKET EXCHANGE SERVICE

Great 42%; good 47%; fair 9%; awful 2%. Comments:
We couldn't buy extra tickets at the exchange. First few days the lines were too long, then later there wasn't anything. One time I sold tickets but I had to do all the work myself. (The exchange was a service, not a hold-your-hand-and-do-all-your-work-for-you operation. If you're not interested enough to wait in line there isn't much we can do for you.)
Closed most of the time we could be there. (Had to be some set hours and you could have made it if you really wanted to.)
Should make purchasers show TAFNOT identification. (No. The tickets were available to everyone. Otherwise TAFNOTers' extra tickets might have gone unsold. Tour members should have preference, however, when there are more buyers than sellers.)
Never used the service. Was too satisfied with my tickets.
Should have allowed seller to recover 50¢ per ticket paid TAFNOT at start. (The 50¢ was paid Ward's, not TAFNOT. And it would be too much of a hassle explaining to buyers why we were collecting more than the face value of the ticket.)
Didn't use. Are you kidding, with our gymnastics and basketball tickets?
Poor organization. Many people were ready to fight. (Sorry about that. We'll try harder next time to eliminate the 11% fair or awful rating.)

TOUR BULLETINS

Great 62%; good 32%; fair 5%; awful .7%. Comments:
Not easily understood. (Tell us where you had trouble and we'll try to do better.)
Bulletins excellent, distribution poor. (? Perhaps you refer to TAFNOT Press, as the bulletins were distributed by mail.)

TAFNOT PRESS

Great 54%; good 41%; fair 5%. Comments:
Hard to find. (You are not alone in this complaint and it must be legitimate. We will have to do better next time. We thought it was going well because we printed 2000 or more each day and they all disappeared somewhere.)

STILL MORE GENERAL COMMENTS

It is the best Olympic tour I have taken. I have found in the past most Olympic tours are very difficult to plan.
Arrangements were perfect. We enjoyed ourselves immensely. I have never had a better time. Have caught the Olympic bug.
I am not much of a joiner but I really liked the way things were made available if and when one wanted.
Excellent. Even my wife doesn't rate "super-fantastic."
Our third tour and you continue to impress us with your attention to important matters and your recognition of the fact we are capable individuals who enjoy taking care of ourselves on a flexible tour.
After reading Garry Hill's article in the September issue we wondered if we were on the same tour. We were not aware of any of those conditions. You people did a hell of a job.
I didn't rate everything excellent because it was too big. There is nothing that can be done about it, but it is better when you are in a workable group as in Mexico City.
No mass operation could have gone much more smoothly. Your backlog of experience has served all of us very well.
We left for Montreal expecting crowds, increased prices, hassles. Instead, we had terrific housing convenient to everything and the crowds and prices were no problem. (We would rather you were prepared for the worst and were pleasantly surprised than vice versa.)

TRADING PINS

Great 17%; good 35%; fair 28%; awful 20%. Comments:
I never received any trading pins, which I understand I should have. (Not necessarily. We should have explained again in the survey. Many people down-rated the trading pins

because they didn't get any. But they weren't supposed to get any. We supplied one souvenir TAFNOT pin per person. Trading pins were *not* part of the basic tour package. We did not include them because many aren't interested and do not wish to pay for them. And there is no way of supplying the desired number for each person who does want them. So we made the trading pins optional. You had the opportunity in October, 1975, to order as many pins as you wanted, of either or both varieties. If you didn't order any, you didn't get any except the one TAFNOT pin which was meant for you, not to trade.)

Rated pin situation awful because neither you nor we fully anticipated needs. (True. Many tour members didn't order when they had the opportunity and then were chagrined, or upset with us, when they later decided they wanted some. Others didn't order enough. Our problem was that the pins had to be ordered well in advance. We got more twice and then again after arrival in Montreal when we bought out the remaining supply of the manufacturer. We fell down by not having enough pins to take care of legitimate needs and messed up on distribution to late joiners, especially.)

I paid for pins and didn't get them. (We're very sorry about that and we've sent out a lot of refund checks. It's a long story, but basically what happened was that when we didn't have enough pins to mail in advance we arranged to deliver in Montreal. We thought we had enough pins to make good on all orders. But then we started selling to others who wanted, even demanded, to buy pins they had not previously ordered. By filling some of those demands we were left short.)

Trading pins should have the year, country and five Olympic rings to make them really worthwhile. (Okay by us. But the only way we can do that is to sell only in advance of departure. We buy 10,000 extra pins, for instance, air freight them to Moscow, pay the duty, and then sell only half or less. What do we do with the left-overs? And if we don't have enough for everyone, who didn't decided in advance, or who needs more, we're in trouble deciding which tour members get the scarce pins.)

Pins are a nuisance and the people who clamor for them are a bigger nuisance. Why don't you forget them entirely. (We would like to. They have been a problem from the beginning. One year the manufacturer failed to produce the pins on time even though ordered a year in advance and it was too late to get any others. In 72 we produced a cheap pin so that everyone could have an ample supply at low cost. Many didn't like the quality.)

Please, either improve on the pin situation or eliminate them. (You are so right. Our most likely solution will be to offer a pin geared to the 1980 Games, available only in advance of departure and not available in Moscow. Plus a timeless Olympic pin that we can sell in Moscow and can be brought back and used in 1984 if unsold. And, oh, please note that the whole disturbing mess is meant to be a service. We sell the pins at cost and do it only for you.)

HAVE YOU SIGNED FOR MOSCOW

We didn't compile the figures although we noted that a substantial majority, perhaps 60%, said they had signed or would sign. We got our answer from a count of the deposits which totaled more than 1200 in the three months from July 15 to October 15. As of late October the count was 2164 and still growing fast. An amazing vote of confidence in TAFNOT and interest in Moscow and the Olympics. On the other hand, the reasons for not going are interesting. Moscow seems to be a place you love to see or hate. Extreme positions are common. Some of the reasons for not going:

Daughter will be in college.
Won't be able to get around by myself very much.
It is Moscow.
Getting a little too old for so far a trip.
Montreal was enough.
Feel that the USSR can't change that much in so short a time.
Too far, too much, and I am too much of a foreigner.
No real good reason.
Still recovering from Montreal.
Language barrier, not much to see, hindered by where you can go and see.
Soviets will not allow freedom of movement. (Many assume this and on past record it is so. However, they promise otherwise.)
Retiring from Olympic attendance.
Probable lack of freedom, low quality food.
Keep American dollars in America. (Or Canada?)
Afraid of poor housing. (We don't know the housing situation yet but chances are there will be no private homes and everyone will be in a hotel of some kind.)
I don't like to patronize with our enemy.
Don't feel Moscow will have the same atmosphere.
Don't care to attend another Olympics.
Too expensive.
Don't like the regime.
Not sure enough of housing set-up. (You can always reserve a place now and cancel if housing is unsatisfactory.)
No desire to go to Russia.
No money.
Would prefer closer site.

INTERNATIONAL JET SETTERS AT MONTREAL
Jo Chez, the Dunmores, and the Waddills./Photo by Fred Chez.

Our religious feelings do not agree with an oppressive country such as the USSR.

My wife doesn't want me to go. I'm henpecked.

Not too sure of treatment and freedom.

Can't plan that far ahead.

Detente, nyet.

Wife not interested. Too expensive unless both can enjoy it.

HOW DO YOU FEEL ABOUT THE PRICE OF THE TOUR?

Bargain 19.3%; just right 74.9%; little high 1.2%; too high 4.6%.

Too high because of Montreal, not TAFNOT. (Several of the few who judged the tour too high expressed this thought and we appreciate it. We're the first to recognize that an average of $18 a track ticket is too high, and that most housing is far overpriced. But we try to hold the price down, providing a fairly priced tour for you and a reasonable profit for us. Apparently we succeed. Your survey response says we do, the repeaters say we do, and comparisons with other tours say we do. Volume helps, of course. A large tour gives us the funds to do things at a per member cost that a small tour couldn't afford.)

In 1972 the response was: bargain 17.2%; just right 69.2%; too high 13.6%. This time we had 94.2% who said just right or bargain, compared with a still good 86.4% in 1976. Interesting, since housing was much higher this time, tickets were up, and there was the high cost of transportation. Undoubtedly the added features of the Hospitality Center, the programs with meals, the TAFNOT Press provided more for your money.

"GOODIES" YOU FEEL ARE NOT WORTH INCLUDING

We reversed the question this time. In 1972 we asked you to indicate those items you liked. Since some skipped the question we couldn't be sure that a non-check meant dislike. This time you had the chance to speak up on the items you feel are not worthwhile. Not worth including: flight bag 11%; cap 18%; Tafnot pin 18%; trading pins 15%; Track & Field News Preview issue 1%; Little Red Book 9%; Olympic Track & Field book 8%; literature on Montreal 2%. Comments:

Second or third time members should have an option on some items. For instance, we may still have our flight bags to use for another tour. (This is a possibility. We will have to give it a lot of thought. More than four out of five want everything. To run the option means not only more paperwork but is bound to create confusion. We can picture tour members storming into our Moscow office demanding the flight bag they never ordered. We'll see.)

Should have had Montreal 76 bag, not old stock. (It wasn't old stock as you will see if you compare bags. It was the same design, however, and we *could* change that.)

Literature on host city should be up to date. (We got the latest they had and don't feel it worthwhile to publish our own.)

AND YET MORE GENERAL COMMENTS

You guys did a great job.

We never had more fun in our lives. There was much, much laughter. I was truly sad on the day we left.

Made me feel like I was in one big happy family.

Everything was more than what you read about or see on TV. Greatest material experience of my life.

Being an organizer myself I felt the overall management and organization for the numbers was commendable.

You have reason to be proud of an enormous undertaking well performed.

My overall rating was lower for Montreal than for Munich for one reason: the Germans were perfect hosts while the Canadians made me feel unwelcome and financially gouged. I will never return to Montreal.

You should be proud of your accomplishments. I don't think any other U.S. tour had so much to offer.

TAFNOT provided everything promised and did so with style. Fox and the staff are to be commended. The Olympics are a great product and TAFNOT does a great job of marketing them.

Superb tour, reasonable priced. Hospitality center was main difference compared to Munich. My fifth TAFNOT adventure and best yet.

You did a heck of a job against the odds the Canadian government threw at you.

I don't doubt your good intentions but you could spend less time congratulating yourselves and put more effort into the tour. Your "comments" were a typical Madison Ave. hype, something I thought Track & Field News was above. In point of fact I heard more complaints than praise. (You can't win them all.)

LIST OTHER ITEMS YOU FEEL SHOULD BE PROVIDED

Daily programs. (It isn't practical for us to do so when they are available in the stadium. True, the $2 price was a rip-off. But we couldn't get the heat assignments, etc., in time to have them printed and distributed in time to be of use.)

More group tours...umbrella...bi-lingual dictionary...flight bag with more compartments...nylon windbreaker...prices on inter-city transportation...calendar of non-Olympic events in city...list and location of campgrounds...location of facilities when ordering tickets...in 1972 we got pens. I used it in 1976 but I don't think it will last until 1980...a world map showing where all the participating countries are located...tie breaking rules for vault, jumps, etc. (they are in the Little Red Book)...you did it all...portable toilet for the women...shade for lower seats...color coded layout of stadium...wallet-sized card on track event schedule...none, but I'll take any and all...

Names and addresses of people on tour. (We don't want to provide a master mailing list that might be abused by others. But if you need address of any new friends, send us a self-addressed stamped envelope.)

Copies of the official press summary with results and entries. (Would be great if we could. We managed to sneak several dozen copies out of the press center each day but couldn't handle thousands.)

Map of the city and transportation info. (We distributed city and subway maps before your departure for Montreal and also had some on hand in Montreal. Apparently not everyone got them, or kept them for later use.)

How to use public transportation; how to avoid rip-offs in taxis; how to get from airport to lodging.

How can you provide any more?

DONATION TO U.S. OLYMPIC COMMITTEE

Would you object to a $10 per person donation to the USOC as part of the tour cost? Yes 19%; no 81%.

I prefer to make my donation with a separate check. (But

you can still take your individual tax deduction when you donate through the tour.)

Doesn't a contribution to the USOC entitle everyone to an Olympic pin or patch? (Yes. We selected the Olympic book. But since a number of people asked about patches we'll probably take that route next time.)

The donation will be siphoned off by the bureaucrats. (Not entirely true. And whether you have good or bad vibes about the USOC you know it takes millions to pay all the Olympic team expenses. And if no one supported the team we wouldn't have much to watch, would we?)

Could be $20 donation.

We didn't even receive an acknowledgement of our $5 donation. (Don't blame the USOC. We didn't send them all the names and told them to save money by not acknowledging each person. The USOC did acknowledge their gratitude to us, very nicely and more than once. The money is most appreciated.)

Federal government should make a greater donation. (They make none now and it's questionable if they should. Anyway, until they do, the USOC has to raise the funds.)

MISCELLANEOUS

I did not like the $7 breakfast-lunch deal. It was difficult to get there and although the meals and conversation were good, $7 was far too much. (Obviously $7 should buy a better meal. But remember that we had to pay the Meridien $75,000 for the use of the Grand Salon. This way we got $60,000 worth of food. It was give you three meals for the $20 or give you nothing, i.e., no hospitality center.)

The meals with speakers were a real plus.

Please move the smokers and other air polluters away from the track fans in the stadium seats. Put them in the bleachers! (It would be great if smokers could be segregated, or if they could be more considerate of their neighbors. It's a problem that bothers more and more people. Even if we could separate our group there is no assurance that a non-TAFNOT stadium neighbor might not smoke. We will give this problem considerable thought.)

How about a pin exchange? (You have to be joshing. We want no more pin headaches. Nothing to keep *you* from organizing one, though.)

Montreal did a very poor job of hosting the Games because of greed and callousness. Montreal is almost as screwed up as New York, Detroit, etc. There's not enough concern for the good of all, just oneself. This was clear in the absurd strikes by the bus company, choosing to strand us folks at MacDonald College. The housing was a downer, but not as much as the covert hostility of the Quebecois toward Anglos.

We needed a check room or lockers. We had a flight bag and three pair of binoculars stolen. (Good suggestion and we'll try to arrange something for Moscow.)

Transfers between airport and housing should receive more attention. (Agree.)

I am not exaggerating when I tell you that my wife and I almost had fist fights with these lowlifes who smoke in the stadium. It is incredible that, in this day and age, in a group of purported track fans, there are individuals who are so inconsiderate. My own theory is that because of the great expansion of TAFNOT there has been included a large number of persons who are not real track people, and who therefore exhibit these anti-social characteristics. (Even some good track fans smoke. But we have noticed the incidence of smokers is considerably less among good track fans.)

We still had trouble meeting people. Maybe group functions rather than meetings.

Travel agency did nothing for us in Montreal. No transportation, no assistance, no nothing.

The Olympic athletes need a whole lot more support. (Then why do you object to including a $10 donation to the USOC?)

Young children should not have been allowed to stay in the hospitality center without supervision.

My only problem was with the travel agency. It would have been just as well to use my local agent.

Having an available medical facility would help. I had a badly infected finger and had a hell of a time finding any treatment.

Another thing that your organization does that is great is answering correspondence quickly. Please never change.

I felt that the tour guide should have taken better care of us as we got off the plane in a strange land. We didn't know where to go or how to get there.

Food will be a major problem in Moscow. Maybe T&FN could provide each tour member with a survival kit of Big Macs.

The inconsideration of camera buffs is becoming more and more noticeable. One man complained loudly about people obstructing his view during the long jump but felt no qualms about doing the same to others during the triple jump. Perhaps all tripods should be banned from the stadium.

Bulletins should give an early definition of what is included in price. (They did. See page 28, in Feb. 1975, before you made your final tour commitment.)

You should recommend that everyone take binoculars. I must have been the only person without them.

Transportation arrangements were so horrible I ended up handling my own.

It would be great if the ticket group could be specified non-smoking. That's honestly the only complaint we can come up with.

Something is needed of a social nature at the beginning of tour to establish friendships for those loners and persons traveling from all points. (That's one of the reasons for the hospitality center.)

The travel bureau is also to be commended. Good flight arrangements and attentive care. To our pleasant surprise we advised them that we would not need transportation to the airport and they promptly refunded half our transfer money. A generous gesture which can only win friends.

I was most disappointed with travel, changing planes and delays when others who joined the tour years later got direct charter flights. (There were no charter flights for anyone.)

At no time did we feel prices were too high. I wish we could get breakfast here for the little we often paid there. We found the quality of food and accommodations excellent throughout.

THE LAST OF THE GENERAL COMMENTS

Thank you for the most wonderful trip and vacation we have ever had. Your planning and programs were the best.

Thank you for what will probably be a once in a lifetime experience.

Your tour was beautiful.

I hate to think what it would have been without the efforts of your whole dedicated staff. Your operation must be a labor of love. (Not entirely. We expect to make a reasonable profit. But we do put a lot of personal dedication into the tours.)

Ed Fox was particularly good.

I can't offer any improvements. I'll recommend your tour to all interested.

The best "tour" I've ever been on. You solved all our problems but did not get in the way. I don't think I'd want to even try the Olympics without your help.

You gave me the best two weeks of my life. It wouldn't have happened without you. Thank you.

I don't care for the paternalistic attitude and the automatic response from tour workers that "here's another coddled American griping." I got sick and tired of hearing you constantly congratulate yourself on how hard you were working and what sacrifices you were making.

In spite of all the inconveniences with housing and tickets and the French-Canadians we enjoyed everything else including the many wonderful people we met. In short, we had a lot of fun despite the rip-offs. Considering grouchy old track nuts, you're doing a hell of a job on the tours.

We old timers dislike seeing the numbers increase but realize that large numbers increase TAFNOT's chances for good seats, housing, etc. Good job as usual.

The courses and speakers were fantastic. I felt thoroughly steeped in Olympic background.

Exhiliratng and fantastic are good descriptive adjectives for your entire everything, from information to tickets to lodging and meeting other nuts like myself.

I can't say enough about the trip. I hope I don't lose any friends with all the talking I've been doing.

The Olympics are truly the greatest show on earth and I have memories I will treasure for the rest of my life. I'm sure that if I had tried to make all the arrangements on my own I would have had many difficulties and would probably have left out many of the non-essentials that made the trip so memorable.

Tafnot 76 was super. Thanks to Garry and Nancy, Jon, Tom, Bert and the rest. It was the trip of a lifetime for myself and son.

Fantastic job you've done. The few problems were obviously not your fault.

This was the best of the last three tours. We're with you for as long as you (or we) last.

The finest thing that has ever happened to me.

Thanks from all the TAFNOT staff:

Bert Nelson	Nancy Hill	Tom Ecker	Pierre Brouillette
Ed Fox	Garry Hill	Jim Santos	Rudy Ligtelyn
Karen Rau	Tom Jordan	Carolyn Santos	Francoise Ardouin
Jim Terrill	Stacey FitzSimmons	George Rhoden	Denise Richards
Jim Renshaw	Don Steffens	Sam Skinner	Pam Miller
JoAnn Renshaw	Cordner Nelson	Geoff Dyson	Molly Newlon
Gerry Daigle	Grace Light	Bertha Light	Patty Schweikert
Sue Mollard	Jon Hendershott		

TAFNOTers and Gold Medalists

Above left, TAFNOT staffers George Rhoden (1952 Olympic 400m. champion), Tom Ecker and Karen Rau. Above right, TAFNOTer Sam Skinner interviews 1976 Olympic discus winner Mac Wilkins. Below left, TAFNOT member Horace Wall with 1968 Olympic long jump history maker Bob Beamon, a frequent visitor to our Hospitality Center. Below right, Peggy Summa and Mary Armstrong, both TAFNOTers. Mary is flashing the gold medal she won as lead-off runner on the victorious 1932 U.S. women's 400m. relay team./Photos by Grace Light, Garry Hill, Horace Wall, and Bill Summa.

Marathoners—including Don Kardong (8) and Bill Rodgers (1)—await the start.

In the rain, it's Frank Shorter in the lead, followed by Singh, Drayton, Viren, Cierpinski and Rodgers.

Paul Geis (US) happily qualifies for the 5000 meter final ahead of Boris Kuznyetsov (USSR) and defending champion Lasse Viren (Finland).

Geis passes the fallen Kuznyetsov in the final.

Poland and West Germany threatened the US as Fred Newhouse began the third leg of the 1600 meter relay.

After Newhouse's 43.8, Maxie Parks had plenty of room to operate on his anchor.

Debra Sapenter (US) 400 meters.

Joni Huntley (US) high jump.

Duncan Macdonald (US) 5000 meters.

Wendy Knudson (US) becomes the second American woman under 2:00 with her 1:59.9 heat effort.

Fred Samara (US) decathlon.

The high hurdles final—Guy Drut (lane 5) champion; Alejandro Casanas (lane 7) second; Willie Davenport (lane 3) third.

From ground level—Charles Foster (4th), Drut, James Owens (6th), Davenport.

Emotion
by Jon Hendershott

The Olympic Games are a gathering and outpouring of emotions as varied as the thousands of individual athletes who compete.

There are the obvious outward signs of release. Victory is smiles, waves, leaps of joy, laps of honor when the athlete can bathe in his brief moment in the warmth of victory.

Defeat is dejection, tears, anger and frustration. That acrid realization of unfulfilled hopes forced to admit to reality.

There are the obvious signs—sometimes.

But the emotions of the Olympics can often be like the Games themselves—unconventional and unpredictable.

* A 1500 meter runner doesn't win his heat—"fails" in the eyes of some—but he has advanced to the semi-finals and he happily points to his time on the scoreboard.

* Jubilant Mike Shine of the US jumps like an excited kangaroo after the 400 meter hurdles —because he has won the silver medal. Teammate Edwin Moses, winner of the gold medal in a world record, is the one who appears reserved.

* Two women finish a 100-meter heat—smiling broadly at each other.

* Moments before the men's 100 final, Valeriy Borzov nervously shakes his arms, Don Quarrie stands impassively with hands on hips and Harvey Glance sits against his lane number pylon, arms

Discus medalist Wilkins (gold), Schmidt (silver), Powell (bronze).

Decathlon bronze medalist Nikolay Avilov—
unbashed mugger.

crossed. Hasely Crawford turns his back to the starting line, rests his arms on the pylon and buries his head. In a matter of seconds, Crawford will win the Olympic championship.

Just as it can be the outward display which shows an athlete's emotion, so can a seemingly expressionless moment.

* After failing to qualify for the javelin final, Richard George sits on a bench and stares at the ground, utterly alone before some 70,000 people.

* A woman finishes her pentathlon 200 meters and walks slowly out of the Olympic arena. She finishes far down the standings, but even competing is a personal triumph.

* American long jumper Larry Myricks slumps against a stadium wall, a blank stare on his face. He has broken an ankle while warming up for the finals. His Olympics for 1976 are over.

* A gathering of marathon runners of every size, shape and description nervously awaits the start, each occupied by his own special thoughts of his own particular mission which lies ahead.

The most beautiful, important and enduring quality about the Games, and the emotions they generate, is that both depend on people. So each Games and each emotion is as unique as each individual.

Determining success and failure are left purely to the individual. Each athlete determines his or her own particular standard of achievement.

The emotions of the athlete reflect how well they live up to their own demands—which are often the most exacting, the most demanding of any expectations.

Each athlete is a unique, individual, special story. So are their emotions. □

"Did I win?" Guy Drut asks the crowd. When it's official, he tells them he did.

800 meter medalists Juantorena (gold), Van Damme (silver), Wohlhuter (bronze).

Gunhild Hoffmeister (East Germany) 1500 meters.

Fernando Mamede (Portugal) 1500 meters.

Craig Virgin (US) 10,000 meters.

James Barrineau (US) High Jump.

Jan Merrill (US) 1500 meters.

Gilles Gemise-Fareau (France) decathlon.

Raelene Boyle (Australia), Linda Haglund (Sweden) 100 meters.

Anders Garderud (Sweden), 3000-meter steeplechase champion.

The Ecstasy—Hasely Crawford (Trinidad) 100 meter champion...

...and the Agony—Daley Thompson (Great Britain) decathlon.

Christine Brehmer (East Germany) 400 meters silver medalist.

Three of East Germany's 400-meter relay champions await the official results: Stecher, Eckert and Bodendorf, with USSR lead-off runner, Tatyana Prorochenko (No. 349).

Repeat double distance champion
Lasse Viren (Finland)
leads Brendan Foster (Great Britain)
in the 10,000 meters *(opposite)*.

Sigrun Siegl (East Germany) pentathlon gold medalist.

Christine Laser (East Germany) pentathlon silver medalist.

Burglinde Pollak (East Germany) pentathlon bronze medalist.

Fred Dixon (US) decathlon.

Guido Kratschmer (West Germany) decathlon silver medalist.

Jacek Wszola (Poland) high jump champion.

The 5000 meters final—Rod Dixon (New Zealand) leads from Knut Kvalheim (Norway), silver medalist Dick Quax (New Zealand), champion Lasse Viren (Finland), bronze medalist Klaus-Peter Hildenbrand (West Germany) and Paul Geis (US).

Viktor Saneyev (USSR) triple jump champion *(opposite)*.

The actual throw, 94.58 meters (310-4) and a world javelin record, for Miklos Nemeth of Hungary.

The final hand-off for the victorious US 400 meter relay team, Millard Hampton to Steve Riddick *(opposite)*.

Henry Marsh (US) steeplechase.

Alberto Juantorena (Cuba), 400-800 champion, winning his first gold medal in the 800 *(opposite)*.

HAPPY HURDLERS—

Edwin Moses (US) embraces teammate
Mike Shine after a world record
400 meter hurdles victory *(opposite)*.
Guy Drut (France) beams after winning the
high hurdles *(right)*.
Johanna Schaller (East Germany) signals
her close 100-meter hurdles triumph
(below).

Don Quarrie (Jamaica) 200 meter champion with silver medalist Millard Hampton (US).

US 1600-meter relay winners Herman Frazier, Fred Newhouse, Benny Brown and Maxie Parks team up for a victory lap *(opposite)*.

Rosalyn Bryant carries the US to the 1600 silver *(below)*.

GIVE 'EM A HAND—
Harvey Glance waves the baton as US mates Johnny Jones, Millard Hampton and Steve Riddick celebrate their 400-meter relay triumph *(above)*.

Frank Shorter greets marathon champion Waldemar Cierpinski (East Germany) *(left)*.

Alberto Juantorena (Cuba) exults after his 400 meter victory from Fred Newhouse and Herman Frazier *(below)*.

Jacek Wszola (Poland) high jump champion

Au revoir, Montreal.

Seconds after the finish of the 400 meters, Irena Szewinska raises her arms in victory.

Not even his own housekeeping efforts could dry the high jump approach enough so Dwight Stones could utilize his speed at take-off. So Stones—who set a world record of 7-7 a month before the Games—was ignominiously reduced to grabbing the bar at a paltry 7-3¾. A week after the Games, he set another world mark (7-7¼).

Stones congratulated victor Jacek Wszola and then acknowledged the cheers (and some boos) of the crowd.

97

Mike Shine (US) 400 meter hurdles silver medalist.

Harvey Glance (US) 100 meters *(opposite)*.

John Walker (New Zealand) 1500 meter champion.

Evelyn Ashford (US) 100 meters.

Herman Frazier to Benny Brown, US 1600 meter relay champions.

Wolfgang Schmidt (East Germany) discus silver medalist *(opposite)*.

Larry Myricks (US) long jump.

Randy Williams (US) long jump silver medalist.

1500 meter heat includes Nina Holmen (Finland), Francie Larrieu (US), Grete Waitz (Norway), and Christiane Stoll (East Germany).

Madeline Jackson (US) 800 meters.

Barbel Eckert (East Germany) 200 meters gold medalist.

Tadeusz Slusarski (Poland) pole vault gold medalist.

Dave Roberts (US) pole vault bronze medalist.

Greg Joy (Canada) high jump silver medalist.

Kate Schmidt (US) javelin bronze medalist.

RESULTS

Men

100 METERS

FINAL (July 24, -0.02)

1. HASELY CRAWFORD (TRIN)	10.06
2. DON QUARRIE (JAM)	10.08
3. VALERIY BORZOV (SU)	10.14
4. HARVEY GLANCE (US)	10.19
5. GUY ABRAHAMS (PAN)	10.25
6. JOHNNY JONES (US)	10.27
7. KLAUS-DIETER KURRAT (EG)	10.31
8. PETAR PETROV (BUL)	10.35

200 METERS

FINAL (July 26, 1.61):

1. DON QUARRIE (JAM)	20.23
2. MILLARD HAMPTON (US)	20.29
3. DWAYNE EVANS (US)	20.43
4. PIETRO MENNEA (IT)	20.54
5. RUY DA SILVA (BRAZ)	20.84
6. BOGDAN GRZEJSZCZAK (POL)	20.91
7. COLIN BRADFORD (JAM)	21.17
8. HASELY CRAWFORD (TRIN)	1:19.6

400 METERS

FINAL (July 29):

1. ALBERTO JUANTORENA (CUB)	44.26
2. FRED NEWHOUSE (US)	44.40
3. HERMAN FRAZIER (US)	44.95
4. FONS BRYDENBACH (BEL)	45.04
5. MAXIE PARKS (US)	45.24
6. RICHARD MITCHELL (AUS)	45.40
7. DAVE JENKINS (GB)	45.57
8. JAN WERNER (POL)	45.63

800 METERS

FINAL (July 25):

1. ALBERTO JUANTORENA (CUB)	1:43.5 WR
2. IVO VAN DAMME (BEL)	1:43.9
3. RICK WOHLHUTER (US)	1:44.1
4. WILLIE WULBECK (WG)	1:45.3
5. STEVE OVETT (GB)	1:45.4
6. LUCIANO SUSANJ (YUG)	1:45.8
7. SRI RAM SINGH (IND)	1:45.8
8. CARLO GRIPPO (IT)	1:48.4

1500 METERS

FINAL (July 31):

1. JOHN WALKER (NZ)	3:39.2
2. IVO VAN DAMME (BEL)	3:39.3
3. PAUL-HEINZ WELLMANN (WG)	3:39.3
4. EAMONN COGHLAN (EIRE)	3:39.5
5. FRANK CLEMENT (GB)	3:39.7
6. RICK WOHLHUTER (US)	3:40.6
7. DAVE MOORCROFT (GB)	3:40.9
8. GRAHAM CROUCH (AUS)	3:41.8
9. JANOS ZEMEN (HUN)	3:43.0

STEEPLECHASE

FINAL (July 28):

1. ANDERS GARDERUD (SWE)	8:08.0 WR
2. BRONISLAW MALINOWSKI (POL)	8:09.2
3. FRANK BAUMGARTL (EG)	8:10.4
4. TAPIO KANTANEN (FIN)	8:12.6
5. MICHAEL KARST (WG)	8:20.2
6. EUAN ROBERTSON (NZ)	8:21.2
7. DAN GLANS (SWE)	8:21.6
8. ANTONIO CAMPOS (SP)	8:22.8

9. Dennis Coates (GB) 8:23.0; 10. Henry Marsh (US) 8:24.0; 11. Tony Staynings (GB) 8:33.7; 12. Ismo Toukonen (Fin) 8:42.7.

5000 METERS

FINAL (July 30):

1. LASSE VIREN (FIN)	13:24.8
2. DICK QUAX (NZ)	13:25.2
3. KLAUS-PETER HILDENBRAND (WG)	13:25.4
4. ROD DIXON (NZ)	13:25.5
5. BRENDAN FOSTER (GB)	13:26.2
6. WILLY POLLEUNIS (BEL)	13:27.0
7. IAN STEWART (GB)	13:27.7
8. ANICETO SIMOES (POR)	13:29.4

9. Knut Kvalheim (Nor) 13:30.3; 10. Detlef Uhlemann (WG) 13:31.1; 11. Enn Sellik (SU) 13:36.7; 12. Paul Geis (US) 13:42.5; 13. Pekka Paivarinta (Fin) 13:46.6;... dnf—Boris Kuznyetsov (SU).

10,000 METERS

FINAL (July 26):

1. LASSE VIREN (FIN)	27:40.4
2. CARLOS LOPES (PORT)	27:45.2
3. BRENDAN FOSTER (GB)	27:54.9
4. TONY SIMMONS (GB)	27:56.3
5. ILIE FLOROIU (RUM)	27:59.9
6. MARIANO HARO (SP)	28:00.3
7. MARC SMET (BEL)	28:02.8
8. BERNIE FORD (GB)	28:17.8

9. Jean-Paul Gomez (Fr) 28:24.2; 10. Jos Hermens (Hol) 28:25.0; 11. Karel Lismont (Bel) 28:26.5; 12. Chris Wardlaw (Aus) 28:29.9; 13. Garry Bjorklund (US) 28:38.1; 14. Dave Fitzsimons (Aus) 29:17.7;... dnf—Emiel Puttemans (Bel) & Knut Boro (Nor).

MARATHON

RESULTS (July 31):

1. WALDEMAR CIERPINSKI (EG)	2:09:55 OR
2. FRANK SHORTER (US)	2:10:46
3. KAREL LISMONT (BEL)	2:11:13
4. DON KARDONG (US)	2:11:16
5. LASSE VIREN (FIN)	2:13:11
6. JEROME DRAYTON (CAN)	2:13:30
7. LEONID MOISEYEV (SU)	2:13:34
8. FRANCO FAVA (IT)	2:14:25

9. Aleksandr Gotskiy (SU) 2:15:34; 10. Henri Schoofs (Bel) 2:15:53; 11. Shivnath Singh (Ind) 2:16:22; 12. Chang Sop Choe (NK) 2:16:34; 13. Massimo Magnani (It) 2:16:57; 14. Goran Bengtsson (Swe) 2:17:40; 15. Kazimierz Orzel (Pol) 2:17:44; 16. Hakan Spik (Fin) 2:17:51; 17. Jack Foster (NZ) 2:17:54; 18. Mario Cuevas (Mex) 2:18:09; 19. Rodolfo Gomez (Mex) 2:18:22;

20. Shigeru So (Japan) 2:18:26; 21. Noriyasu Mizukami (Japan) 2:18:45; 22. Anacletto Pinto (Por) 2:18:54; 23. Jose de Jesus (PR) 2:19:35; 24. Yuriy Velikhorodnikh (SU) 2:19:46; 25. Jos Hermens (Hol) 2:19:49; 26. Jeff Norman (GB) 2:20:05; 27. Jukka Toivola (Fin) 2:20:27; 28. Jorgen Jensen (Den) 2:20:45; 29. Michail Kousis (Gr) 2:21:42;

30. Tom Howard (Can) 2:22:09; 31. Keith Angus (GB) 2:22:19; 32. Akio Usami (Japan) 2:22:30; 33. Rigoberto Mendoza (Cub) 2:22:44; 34. Fernand Kolbeck (Fr) 2:22:57; 35. Chris Wardlaw (Aus) 2:23:57.

20-KILO WALK

RESULTS (July 23):

1. DANIEL BAUTISTA (MEX)	1:24:41
2. HANS-GEORG REIMANN (EG)	1:25:14
3. PETER FRENKEL (EG)	1:25:30
4. KARL-HEINZ STADTMULLER (EG)	1:26:51
5. RAUL GONZALES (MEX)	1:28:19
6. ARMANDO ZAMBALDO (ITALY)	1:28:26
7. VLADIMIR GOLUBNICHIY (SU)	1:29:25
8. VITTORIO VISINI (ITALY)	1:29:32

9. Gerard Lelievre (Fr) 1:29:54; 10. Roberto Buccione (It) 1:30:40; 11. Brian Adams (GB) 1:30:47; 12. Ross Haywood (Aus) 1:31:00; 13. Otto Bartsch (SU) 1:31:13; 14. Ollie Flynn (GB) 1:31:43; 15. Viktor Semyenov (SU) 1:31:59; 16. Imre Stankovics (Hun) 1:32:07; 17. Jan Ornoch (Pol) 1:32:20; 18. Gerhard Weidner (WG) 1:32:57; 19. Ernesto Beruudez (Col) 1:33:14.

110 HURDLES

FINAL (July 28):

1. GUY DRUT (FRANCE)	13.30
2. ALEJANDRO CASANAS (CUBA)	13.33
3. WILLIE DAVENPORT (US)	13.38
4. CHARLES FOSTER (US)	13.41
5. THOMAS MUNKELT (EG)	13.44
6. JAMES OWENS (US)	13.73
7. VYACHESLAV KULEBYAKIN (SU)	13.93
8. VIKTOR MYASNIKOV (SU)	13.94

400 HURDLES

FINAL (July 25):

1. EDWIN MOSES (US)	47.64WR
2. MIKE SHINE (US)	48.69
3. YEVGENIY GAVRILYENKO (SU)	49.45
4. QUENTIN WHEELER (US)	49.86
5. JOSE CARVALHO (PORT)	49.94
6. YANKO BRATANOV (BUL)	50.03
7. ALFONSO DAMASO (CUBA)	50.19
8. ALAN PASCOE (GB)	51.29

HIGH JUMP

FINAL (July 31):

1. JACEK WSZOLA (POL)	2.25	7-4½OR
2. GREG JOY (CAN)	2.23	7-3¾
3. DWIGHT STONES (US)	2.21	7-3
4. SERGEY BUDALOV (SU)	2.21	7-3
5. SERGEY SENYUKOV (SU)	2.18	7-1¾
6. RODOLFO BERGAMO (ITALY)	2.18	7-1¾
7. ROLF BEILSCHMIDT (EG)	2.18	7-1¾
8. JESPER TORRING (DEN)	2.18	7-1¾

9. Terje Totland (Nor) 7-1¾; 10. Rune Almen (Swe) 7-1¾; 11. James Barrineau (US) 7-¼; 12. Claude Ferragne (Can) 7-¼; 13. Bill Jankunis (US) 6-10¾; 14. Leif-Roar Falkum (Nor) 6-10¾.

POLE VAULT

FINAL (July 26):

1. TADEUSZ SLUSARSKI (POL)	5.50	18-½=OR
2. ANTTI KALLIOMAKI (FIN)	5.50	18-½=OR
3. DAVE ROBERTS (US)	5.50	18-½=OR
4. PATRICK ABADA (FR)	5.45	17-10½
5. WOJCIECH BUCIARSKI (POL)	5.45	17-10½
6. EARL BELL (US)	5.45	17-10½
7. JEAN-MICHEL BELLOT (FR)	5.40	17-8½
8. ITSUO TAKANEZAWA (JAPAN)	5.40	17-8½

9. Gunther Lohre (WG) 17-6¾; 10. Yuriy Prokhoryenko (SU) 17-2¾; 11. Wladyslaw Kozakiewicz (Pol) 17-2¾; 12. Don Baird (Aus) 17-2¾; 13. tie, Vladimir Kishkun (SU) & Terry Porter (US) 17-¾; 15. Tapani Haapakoski (Fin) 17-¾; 16. Brian Hooper (GB) 16-5.

LONG JUMP

FINAL (July 29):

1. ARNIE ROBINSON (US)	8.35	27-4¾
2. RANDY WILLIAMS (US)	8.11	26-7¼
3. FRANK WARTENBERG (EG)	8.02	26-3¾
4. JACQUES ROUSSEAU (FR)	8.00	26-3
5. JOAO OLIVIERA (BRAZ)	8.00	26-3
6. NENAD STEKIC (YUG)	7.89	25-10¾
7. VALERIY PODLUZHNIY (SU)	7.88	25-10¼
8. HANS BAUMGARTNER (WG)	7.84	25-8¾

9. Rolf Bernhard (Switz) 25-4¾; 10. Aleksey Pereverzyev (SU) 25-1½; 11. Fletcher Lewis (Bah) 24-11¾.

TRIPLE JUMP

FINAL (July 30):

1. VIKTOR SANEYEV (SU)	17.29	56-8¾
2. JAMES BUTTS (US)	17.18	56-4½
3. JOAO OLIVEIRA (BRAZ)	16.90	55-5½
4. PEDRO PEREZ (CUBA)	16.81	55-1¾
5. TOMMY HAYNES (US)	16.78	55-¾
6. WOLFGANG KOLMSEE (WG)	16.68	54-8¾
7. EUGENIUS BISKUPSKI (POL)	16.49	54-1¼
8. CAROL CORBU (RUM)	16.43	53-11

9. Jiri Vycichlo (Cze) 53-5; 10. Pentti Kuukasjarvi (Fin) 53-3; 11. Bernard Lamitie (Fr) 53-3; 12. Rayfield Dupree (US) 53-3.

SHOT PUT

FINAL (July 24):

1. UDO BEYER (EG)	21.05	69-¾
2. YEVGENIY MIRONOV (SU)	21.03	69-0
3. ALEKSANDR BARISHNIKOV (SU)	21.00	68-10¾
4. AL FEUERBACH (US)	20.55	67-5
5. HANS-PETER GIES (EG)	20.47	67-2
6. GEOFF CAPES (GB)	20.36	66-9½
7. GEORGE WOODS (US)	20.26	66-5¾
8. HANS HOGLUND (SWE)	20.17	66-2

9. Pete Shmock (US) 65-3; 10. Heinz-Joachim Rothenburg (EG) 64-11¼; 11. Jaroslav Brabec (Cze) 64-4½; 12. Reijo Stahlberg (Fin) 62-3¾.

DISCUS

FINAL (July 25):

1. MAC WILKINS (US)	67.50	221-5
2. WOLFGANG SCHMIDT (EG)	66.22	217-3
3. JOHN POWELL (US)	65.70	215-7
4. NORBERT THIEDE (EG)	64.30	210-11
5. SIEGFRIED PACHALE (EG)	64.24	210-9
6. PENTTI KAHMA (FIN)	63.12	207-1
7. KNUT HJELTNES (NOR)	63.06	206-11
8. JAY SILVESTER (US)	61.98	203-4

9. Ludvik Danek (Cze) 201-0; 10. Velko Velev (Bul) 199-11; 11. Ferenc Tegla (Hun) 198-7; 12. Hein-Direck Neu (WG) 198-4; 13. Jozef Silhavy (Cze) 191-8

HAMMER

28):

BYEDIKH (SU)	77.52	254-4 OR
EY SPIRIDONOV (SU)	76.08	249-7
OLIY BONDARCHUK (SU)	75.48	247-8
HANS RIEHM (WG)	75.46	247-7
TER SCHMIDT (WG)	74.72	245-2
IEN SACHSE (EG)	74.30	243-9
IIS BLACK (GB)	73.18	240-1
WIN KLEIN (WG)	71.34	234-1

Jacques Accambray (Fr) 231-1; 10. Manfred Seidel 229-9; 11. Shigenobu Murofushi (Japan) 226-0; 12. Farmer (Aus) 223-1.

JAVELIN

AL (July 26):

MIKLOS NEMETH (HUN)	94.58	310-4 WR
HANNU SIITONEN (FIN)	87.92	288-5
GHEORGHE MEGELEA (RUM)	87.16	285-11
PJOTR BIELCZYK (POL)	86.50	283-9
SAM COLSON (US)	86.16	282-8
VASILIY YERSHOV (SU)	85.26	279-9
SEPPO HOVINEN (FIN)	84.26	276-5
. JANIS LUSIS (SU)	80.26	263-4

9. Michael Wessing (WG) 259-4; 10. Terje Thorslund 'or) 256-8; 11. Phil Olsen (Can) 254-11; 12. Amado orales (PR) 247-10; 13. Bjorn Grimnes (Nor) 245-8.

DECATHLON

RESULTS (July 29-30):

1. BRUCE JENNER (US) 8618 WR (4298 [3], 4320)
   10.94 23-8¼ 50-4¼ 6-8 47.51
   14.84 164-2 15-9 224-9 4:12.6
2. GUIDO KRATSCHMER (WG) 8411 (4333 [1], 4078)
   10.66 24-3 48-4¼ 6-8 48.19
   14.58 149-11 15-1¼ 217-5 4:29.1
3. NIKOLAY AVILOV (SU) 8369 (4315 [2], 4054)
   11.23 24-8 48-7 7-¼ 48.16
   14.20 149-7 14-7¾ 204-3 4:26.3
4. RAIMO PIHL (SWE) 8218 (4216 [4], 4002)
   10.93 22-11¼ 51-¼ 6-6¾ 47.97
   15.81 145-4 14-5¾ 253-9 4:28.8
5. RYS. SKOWRONEK (POL) 8113 (4066 [10], 4047)
   11.02 23-9¾ 45-1 6-3¼ 47.91
   14.75 148-9 15-9 204-1 4:29.9
6. SIEGFRIED STARK (EG) 8048 (3956 [14], 4092)
   11.35 22-10¾ 49-5¾ 6-3¼ 49.14
   15.65 149-2 15-3 243-4 4:24.9
7. LEONID LITVINYENKO (SU) 8025 (3978 [12], 4047)
   11.12 22-8½ 46-7 6-3¼ 48.44
   14.72 151-9 15-1¼ 176-1 4:11.4
8. LENNART HEDMARK (SWE) 7974 (3938 [15], 4036)
   11.36 23-3¼ 49-2½ 6-3¼ 49.80
   14.79 152-3 14-1¼ 257-10 4:44.3

9. Aleksandr Grebenyuk (SU) 7803 (11.10, 21-5, 48-2¼, 6-5½, 49.21 [3944—14], 15.05, 154-8, 13-1½, 224-4, 4:39.6 [3809]); 10. Klaus Marek (WG) 7767 (10.81, 21-5½, 44-¼, 6-3¼, 47.12 [4133—7], 15.19, 126-0, 14-1½, 171-8, 4:27.8 [3634]); 11. Johannes Lahti (Fin) 7711 (10.89, 21-6¼, 44-9½, 6-6¾, 49.34 [4109—9], 15.31, 126-4, 13-9½, 202-4, 4:45.9 [3602]); 12. Ryszard Katus (Pol) 7616 (11.06, 23-1¼, 44-2¼, 6-½, 49.87 [3839—19], 14.51, 145-2, 14-9¼, 188-9, 4:47.0 [3777]).

400-METER RELAY

FINAL (July 31):

1. **UNITED STATES** **38.33**
   (Glance, Jones, Hampton, Riddick)
2. **EAST GERMANY** **38.66**
   (Kokot, Pfeifer, Kurrat, Thieme)
3. **USSR** **38.78**
   (Aksinin, Kolesnikov, Silovs, Borzov)
4. **POLAND** **38.83**
   (Swierczynski, Woronin, Grzejszczak, Licznerski)
5. **CUBA** **39.01**
   (Gomez, Casanas, Ramirez, Leonard)
6. **ITALY** **39.08**
   (Guerini, Caravani, Benedetti, Mennea)
7. **FRANCE** **39.16**
   (Amoureux, Arame, Sainte-Rose, Chauvelot)
8. **CANADA** **39.47**
   (Spooner, Nash, Dukowski, Fraser)

1600-METER RELAY

FINAL (July 31):

1. UNITED STATES 2:58.7
   (Frazier 45.3, Brown 44.6, Newhouse 43.8, Parks 45.0)
2. POLAND 3:01.4
   (Podlas 46.7, Werner 44.0, Jaremski 45.5, Pietrzyk 45.2)
3. WEST GERMANY 3:02.0
   (Hofmeister 46.0, Krieg 45.3, Schmid 45.8, Herrmann 44.9)
4. CANADA 3:02.6
   (Seale 47.0, Domansky 45.3, Hope 45.5, Saunders 44.8)
5. JAMAICA 3:02.8
   (Priestley 46.4, Bradford 46.3, Daley 46.3, Newman 43.8)
6. TRINIDAD 3:03.5
   (Solomon 46.0, Tuitt 45.4, Coombs 46.4, Joseph 45.9)
7. CUBA 3:03.8
   (Gutierrez 46.0, Damaso 46.7, Alvarez 46.4, Juanto 44.7)
8. FINLAND 3:06.5
   (Makela 46.3, Karttunen 46.7, Lonnqvist 46.9, Kukk 46.6)

Women

100 METERS

FINAL (July 25, 0.0):

1.	ANNEGRET RICHTER (WG)	11.08
2.	RENATE STECHER (EG)	11.13
3.	INGE HELTEN (WG)	11.17
4.	RAELENE BOYLE (AUS)	11.23
5.	EVELYN ASHFORD (US)	11.24
6.	CHANDRA CHEESEBOROUGH (US)	11.31
7.	ANDREA LYNCH (GB)	11.32
8.	MARLIES OELSNER (EG)	11.34

200 METERS

FINAL (July 28, 0.0):

1.	BARBEL ECKERT (EG)	22.37 OR
2.	ANNEGRET RICHTER (WG)	22.39
3.	RENATE STECHER (EG)	22.47
4.	CARLA BODENDORF (EG)	22.64
5.	INGE HELTEN (WG)	22.68
6.	TATYANA PROROCHENKO (SU)	23.03
7.	DENISE ROBERTSON (AUS)	23.05
8.	CHANTAL REGA (FR)	23.09

400 METERS

FINAL (July 29):

1.	IRENA SZEWINSKA (POL)	49.29 WR
2.	CHRISTINE BREHMER (EG)	50.51
3.	ELLEN STREIDT (EG)	50.55
4.	PIRJO HAGGMAN (FIN)	50.56
5.	ROSALYN BRYANT (US)	50.65
6.	SHEILA INGRAM (US)	50.90
7.	RIITTA SALIN (FIN)	50.98
8.	DEBRA SAPENTER (US)	51.66

800 METERS

FINAL (July 26):

1.	TATYANA KAZANKINA (SU)	1:54.9 WR
2.	NIKOLINA SHTEREVA (BUL)	1:55.4
3.	ELFI ZINN (EG)	1:55.6
4.	ANITA WEISS (EG)	1:55.7
5.	SVYETLANA STYRKINA (SU)	1:56.4
6.	SVETLA KOLEVA (BUL)	1:57.2
7.	DORIS GLUTH (EG)	1:59.0
8.	MARIANA SUMAN (RUM)	2:02.2

1500 METERS

FINAL (July 30):

1.	TATYANA KAZANKINA (SU)	4:05.5
2.	GUNHILD HOFFMEISTER (EG)	4:06.0
3.	ULRIKE KLAPEZYNSKI (EG)	4:06.1
4.	NIKOLINA SHTEREVA (BUL)	4:06.6
5.	LYUDMILA BRAGINA (SU)	4:07.2
6.	GABRIELLA DORIO (IT)	4:07.3
7.	ELLEN WELLMANN (WG)	4:07.9
8.	JAN MERRILL (US)	4:08.5
9.	NINA HOLMEN (FIN)	4:10.0

100-METER HURDLES

FINAL (July 29, 0.0):

1.	JOHANNA SCHALLER (EG)	12.77
2.	TATYANA ANISIMOVA (SU)	12.78
3.	NATALYA LEBEDYEVA (SU)	12.80
4.	GUDRUN BEREND (EG)	12.82
5.	GRAZYNA RABSZTYN (POL)	12.96
6.	ESTHER ROT (ISR)	13.04
7.	VALERIA STEFANESCU (RUM)	13.35
8.	ILEANA ONGAR (IT)	13.51

HIGH JUMP

FINAL (July 28):

1.	ROSEMARIE ACKERMANN (EG)	1.93	6-4 OR
2.	SARA SIMEONI (IT)	1.91	6-3¼
3.	YORDANKA BLAGOYEVA (BUL)	1.91	6-3¼
4.	MARIA MRACNOVA (CZECH)	1.89	6-2½
5.	JONI HUNTLEY (US)	1.89	6-2½
6.	TATYANA SHLYAKHTO (SU)	1.87	6-1¾
7.	ANNETTE TANNANDER (SWE)	1.87	6-1¾
8.	CORNELIA POPA (RUM)	1.87	6-1¾

9. Andrea Matay (Hun) 6-1¾; 10. Julie White (Can) 6-1¾; 11. Brigitte Holzapfel (WG) 6-1¾.

LONG JUMP

FINAL (July 23):

1.	ANGELA VOIGT (EG)	6.72	22-½
2.	KATHY MC MILLAN (US)	6.66	21-10¼
3.	LIDIYA ALFEYEVA (SU)	6.60	21-7¾
4.	SIGRUN SIEGL (EG)	6.59	21-7½
5.	ILDIKA ERDELYI (HUN)	6.57	21-6¾
6.	JARMILA NYGRYNOVA (CZECH)	6.54	21-5½
7.	HEIDE WYCISK (EG)	6.39	20-11½
8.	ELENA VINTILA (RUM)	6.38	20-11¼

SHOT PUT

RESULTS (July 31):

1.	IVANKA KHRISTOVA (BUL)	21.16	69-5 OR
2.	NADYEZHDA CHIZOVA (SU)	20.96	68-9¼
3.	HELENA FIBINGEROVA (CZECH)	20.67	67-9¾
4.	MARIANNE ADAM (EG)	20.55	67-5
5.	ILONA SCHOKNECHT (EG)	20.54	67-4¾
6.	MARGITTA DROESE (EG)	19.79	64-11¼
7.	EVA WILMS (WG)	19.29	63-3½
8.	ELENA STOYANOVA (BUL)	18.89	61-11¾

9. Esfir Krachevskaya (SU) 60-2¾; 10. Faina Myelnik (SU) 59-3½; 11. Maria Sarria (Cub) 53-6¼; 12. Maren Seidler (US) 51-2¼; 13. Lucette Moreau (Can) 50-9½. (No qualifying round was held.)

DISCUS

FINAL (July 29):

1.	EVELYN SCHLAAK (EG)	69.00	226-4 OR
2.	MARIA VERGOVA (BUL)	67.30	220-9
3.	GABRIELLE HINZMANN (EG)	66.84	219-3
4.	FAINA MYELNIK (SU)	66.40	217-10
5.	SABINE ENGEL (EG)	65.88	216-2
6.	ARGENTINA MENIS (RUM)	65.38	214-6
7.	MARIA BETANCOURT (CUBA)	63.86	209-6
8.	NATALYA GORBACHOVA (SU)	63.46	208-2

JAVELIN

FINAL (July 24):

1.	RUTH FUCHS (EG)	65.94	216-4 OR
2.	MARION BECKER (WG)	64.70	212-3
3.	KATE SCHMIDT (US)	63.96	209-10
4.	JACQUELINE HEIN (EG)	63.84	209-5
5.	SABINE SEBROWSKI (EG)	63.08	206-11
6.	SVYETLANA BABICH (SU)	59.42	194-11
7.	NADYEZHDA YAKUBOVICH (SU)	59.16	194-1
8.	KARIN SMITH (US)	57.50	188-8

9. Eva Janko (Aut) 187-8; 10. Theresa Sanderson (GB) 187-0; 11. Eva Zorgo (Rum) 182-5; 12. Yordanka Peeva (Bul) 171-5.

PENTATHLON

RESULTS (July 25-26):

1. SIGRUN SIEGL (EG) 4745
   (13.31, 42-4¾, 5-8½, 51-3½, 23.09)
2. CHRISTINE LASER (EG) 4745
   (13.55, 46-10½, 5-10, 20-7, 23.48)
3. BURGLINDE POLLAK (EG) 4740
   (13.30, 53-3¾, 5-4½, 20-8, 23.64)
4. LYUDMILA POPOVSKAYA (SU) 4700
   (13.33, 49-3¾, 5-8½, 20-3¾, 24.10)
5. NADYEZHDA TKACHENKO (SU) 4669
   (13.41, 48-10¾, 5-11, 19-11½, 24.61)
6. DIANE JONES (CAN) 4582
   (13.79, 47-10, 5-11, 20-7¾, 25.33)
7. JANE FREDERICK (US) 4566
   (13.54, 47-8¾, 5-9¼, 19-7¾, 24.70)
8. MARGIT PAPP (HUN) 4535
   (14.14, 48-6¾, 5-10, 20-10, 25.43)

9. Penka Sokolova (Bul) 4394 (13.32, 44-11½, 5-4½, 19-5½, 24.95); 10. Margot Eppinger (WG) 4352 (13.97, 41-10, 5-6¼, 19-11, 24.61).

400-METER RELAY

FINAL (July 31):

1. EAST GERMANY 42.55 OR
   (Oelsner, Stecher, Bodendorf, Eckert)
2. WEST GERMANY 42.59
   (Possekel, Helten, Richter, Kroniger)
3. USSR 43.09
   (Prorochenko, Maslakova, Besfamilnaya, Anisimova)
4. CANADA 43.17
   (Howe, Loverock, McTaggart, Bailey)
5. AUSTRALIA 43.18
   (Wilson, Wells, Robertson, Boyle)
6. JAMAICA 43.24
   (Hodges, Allwood, Cummings, Pusey)
7. UNITED STATES 43.35
   (Watson, Ashford, Armstrong, Cheeseborough)
8. GREAT BRITAIN 43.79
   (Clarke, Ramsden, Colyear, Lynch)

1600-METER RELAY

FINAL (July 31):

1. EAST GERMANY 3:19.2WR
   (Maletzki 50.5, Rohde 49.5, Streidt 49.5, Brehmer 49.7)
2. UNITED STATES 3:22.8
   (Sapenter 51.8, Ingram 50.0, Jiles 51.3, Bryant 49.7)
3. SOVIET UNION 3:24.2
   (Klimovicha 51.4, Aksenova, Sokolova, Ilyina)
4. AUSTRALIA 3:25.6
   (Canty 52.4, Burnard 51.2, Rendina 51.6, Nail 50.4)
5. WEST GERMANY 3:25.7
   (Steger 52.4, Fuhrmann 51.3, Barth 51.5, Wilden 50.5)
6. FINLAND 3:25.9
   (Lindholm 52.8, Haggman 51.4, Pursiainen 52.0, Salin 50.6)
7. GREAT BRITAIN 3:28.0
   (Barnes 52.5, Taylor 52.6, Elder 52.6, Murray 50.3)
8. CANADA 3:28.9
   (Stride 53.1, Yakubowich 51.6, Campbell 52.5, Saunders 51.7)